Taking Dictation

Attuning Your Ear to the Voice of God

Ralph Hale

INDIA • SINGAPORE • MALAYSIA

Notion Press

No.8, 3rd Cross Street
CIT Colony, Mylapore
Chennai, Tamil Nadu – 600004

First Published by Notion Press 2021
Copyright © Ralph Hale 2021
All Rights Reserved.

ISBN 978-1-63806-673-6

To Vicki

My opposite, my editor, and my love

Cover design
by
Erin Pritchard

Contents

Chapter One

Why Don't We Hear God's Voice Anymore?

As I looked over the crowd of young exuberant first-generation Russian Christians, my attention was arrested by an incongruous sight: a stern-faced older Russian man in an ill-fitting Soviet-era suit and a briefcase balanced on his knees… it was Professor Peacmonik! I had already encountered "The Professor" several times in our first year of trying to plant a church in the industrial city of Perm, Russia. He had a dark history from the Soviet days and was well-known to the older believers in our city as an expert on Christianity, with no love for Christians. He was the head of the "Religious Affairs Committee" and I had nervously sat before that committee for several months as they reviewed my application to officially register the church. In those days, just six years since the collapse of the Soviet Union, non-Orthodox churches were treated with great suspicion by the government. We were lumped together with all of the cults in the world (our church happened to be on the docket along with Scientology) and they were determined to make it as hard as possible to start a church in their city.

Even though the professor was no friend to Christians, I learned after our first meeting that he knew much more Christian theology than I did! As he carefully questioned me and even set up a few clever theological traps, I realized I was in the presence of someone much smarter than I. My strategy was to simply be as honest and open as I could be without pretending to be someone that I wasn't. He had been promising for some time to visit our Sunday service, but it was still a shock to see him sitting there – right at the end of a three-day worship conference no less!

After the service, he asked to speak to me privately, and as I steeled myself for the worst, I saw him smile (for what I think was the first time) as he said: "We have decided to give you your church registration." As I reached out to shake his hand in gratitude, he stopped me with his next sentence, "This registration has one condition, you must be willing to keep your church within the city limits of Perm and not spread your work into other parts of the region." I really didn't know how to respond and I found that all I could do was to ask him to give me a week to think about it. We agreed to meet at the beginning of the next month at the next gathering of the Religious Affairs Committee. As he left the building, I asked some of the businesspeople that came to our church what they thought I should do. They were unanimous, "Take the registration now and work on changing the conditions later, that's the Russian way." As a brand-new church planter who was still learning the Russian culture, I was tempted to follow their advice – but I had one more place that I could turn to, my prayer journal!

I had been seriously keeping a prayer journal for about ten years at that point. It contained not only Scripture I was meditating on but also what I felt God was saying to me through that Scripture to my heart. I went home and pulled out my journal for that year and began to carefully read over the pages one by one. As I closed the journal, I was amazed at how often God had spoken to me that year about our church: that it was to be an outwardly focused church and a platform for sending church planters into other Russian cities and even other nations. There was also something else that was surprising, as I closed my journal that evening; I realized that I knew the answer that I had to give to Professor Peacmonik – and that answer was, "No!" More than thirty times in my journal God had spoken about our church and its mission's call, so to accept his condition would have been to ignore what God had been consistently saying to me all year.

As I came to the next meeting of the Religious Affairs Committee, along with a translator and some Russian members of my leadership team, I was surprised when the professor stood up and gave a very positive and fair evaluation of our church. At the end of his address, he casually mentioned that we were also willing to accept the condition laid down by the committee as he prepared to call the vote… at that point, I realized that I was going to interrupt "The Professor"! I don't think he had been interrupted many times in his life, but after he grudgingly yielded me the floor, I started to share, through my translator, a short explanation of the Great Commission that Jesus gave to his church, "Go into all the world and preach the gospel." At the end of my little talk, I then said with great fear and trembling, "Because of the words of Jesus, we respectfully decline the registration if it must contain this condition." I had a scary glimpse of the man I had heard about in Soviet times as he angrily stood up and demanded that we leave the room. As we meekly sat on a bench out in the hall, it was probably the lowest point of my brand-new church planting career. Registration with the government in those days was absolutely essential if a new church was going to rent a public hall or have meetings in public places. I wasn't sure what we would do without it. As they came out and informed us to come back next month, I went home with very mixed feelings: I didn't have the registration, but I had made the right decision based on what we felt God was saying.

The next month we returned to the Religious Affairs Committee, and to my surprise, another committee member stood to give us their decision. As I looked over at "The Professor," he wouldn't make eye contact and looked angry; but as his assistant began to speak, I heard the words that would set the future direction of our church for the next twenty years, "We have decided to give you your registration without conditions!"

Looking back on that day, as we went home on the bus rejoicing, I realize how close I had come to making a very serious mistake in the planting of that young church. If I had been willing to accept the condition and limit growth only to our local church in the city of Perm, I would have set a precedent that could have easily been used against the many other churches that were coming into our city in those days. Even more seriously, it's possible that a conditional registration might have aborted the future church that God would later birth through us in the autonomous Muslim city of Ufa – all of which could have been very different had I not had a way of remembering what God had already said!

That incident in Russia was the beginning of a major discovery in my life as a Christian: the realization that God is speaking all the time! In the next few years, as many young Russians came to Christ and I slowly began to develop national leaders, it became a normal way of life in our church to listen to God each morning and keep a record of what he was saying.

After returning to the United States in 2009, along with the reverse culture shock of re-entering the land of Walmart and fast food, we were also truly surprised at how few Christians (even pastors and leaders) practiced listening to God each morning. Most people we met would read their Bible in the morning and some would write down their prayers to God, but almost no one lived as though they believed that God wanted to talk back! In our private times together, my wife and I would ask each other, "Why do people believe that God doesn't speak anymore?"

God Spoke to the First Church

In the New Testament, the willingness of God the Father to speak to his children was one of the defining characteristics of this new sect called Christianity. On almost the first day of the church, after the Holy Spirit had come down with tongues of fire on the heads of the apostles and they started to speak in other languages, Peter immediately explained this phenomenon in the context of God speaking. Quoting a famous prophecy by the Old Testament prophet Joel, Peter said, "In the last days, God says, I will pour out my spirit on all people your sons and daughters will prophesy, your young men will see visions, your old men will dream dreams. Even on my servants, both men and women, I will pour out my spirit in those days, and they will prophesy" (Acts 2:17-18).

I've always found it significant that Peter didn't explain this astounding sight of the manifestation of the Holy Spirit as something delegated only to the eleven disciples. He made it plain that God would speak to and through *all* people, including young people and old people and servants and women, as well as men! That word "prophesy" has become so glamorized and stigmatized that we think it doesn't apply to the average Christian, but from the very first day of the church, Peter made it clear that prophecy, God speaking to and through people, was meant to be a common occurrence in the lives of all Christians whatever their age, or education, or status in life.

Throughout the story of the first church, we find examples of how decisions were made, and how the course of the church was changed according to what God was saying. Saul, the great persecutor of the church who became a Christian, did not decide to follow Jesus because of someone's logical gospel presentation – God spoke directly to his heart! After getting up from having fallen off his horse, he heard the Lord say, "Saul, Saul why do you persecute me?" When Saul asked who was speaking to him, the Lord replied, "I am Jesus whom you are persecuting, now get up and go into the city and you will be told what you must do" (Acts 9:4-6). We forget that it was Saul's decision to believe that he was hearing from God and his determination to obey what he was hearing that changed not only the course of his life but also the course of much of the Christian theology that was to come.

It was a decision based on what God was saying, not a clever plan for church expansion, that caused the church of the first century to begin embracing Gentiles and even members of the Roman society who oppressed them. When Peter had the vision of a large sheet being let down to the Earth filled with all kinds of "unclean" animals, God spoke to his heart and said, "Do not call anything impure that God has made clean" (Acts 10:15). Interestingly, God had to speak to him multiple times before he had the courage and the faith-level he needed to break every precedent and go to the house of Cornelius a Roman officer over the Italian Regiment! The Christian church could have easily been just a subset of Judaism if Peter had not been willing to give time to God that morning and then lead the church in the direction that God was speaking to him.

When you look for the evidence of God speaking in the Book of Acts, it's clear that God directed almost every part of the development and the expansion of the early church. Not only denying entrance (for a time) to Paul and his companions into the province of Asia, but also speaking to everyday believers who warned Paul what he would be facing in Jerusalem. The more that you read the story of the first church, the more you get the feeling that perhaps we have lost something in the 21st century that was much more common to Christians in the 1st Century. So, what causes Christians to believe that God isn't speaking anymore?

It's Hard to Hear in a Crowded Room

It's almost a cliché these days to talk about all of the "voices" that clamor to be heard in our modern society: the television shouts the local news when we get up in the morning, the radio sings to us on the drive to work, and our days are filled with our bosses' demands and our children's questions – we truly live in a crowded room! But strangely, it seems that God has mostly chosen to speak to us in a still small voice, despite the fact that small voices so often get drowned out by big voices in the world. Many Christians have lost the ability to, as Jesus said, go into the "inner room" and find a quiet place away from all the other voices in their lives. Because we don't actively and consistently seek out a quiet place where we can hear his voice, we draw the wrong conclusion: that God really doesn't speak to the average person.

Very early in my life as a Christian, as I was attempting to live in the slums of the Philippines in the 1980s with a young church and a tiny health clinic reaching out to an extremely poor population, I came to a place personally where I was pretty much overwhelmed by all of the voices of the needy that assailed our inexperienced team every day. People lined up each morning outside our door with horrific needs, and our congregation was composed of mostly first-generation Christians who needed a lot of attention. It reached the point where I wondered if I were experiencing "burnout" and entertained the embarrassing notion that I needed a long vacation after only one year on the job. One morning, instead of going about business as usual, I managed to go into a quiet place in my small room and open my ears to the Father; almost immediately God's word leapt into my heart, "Are you so foolish? After beginning by means of the spirit, are you now trying to finish by means of the flesh?" (Galatians 3:3). With that one clear word from God, I was able to reorder my personal life and continue that ministry in the same way I had started it, in complete dependence on God's Spirit. The problem was not that God wasn't speaking, it was that in the "crowded room" of good deeds and missionary work I was unable to hear him. Unfortunately, so often we tend to turn up the volume of our lives when we are feeling overwhelmed instead of dialing down into a quiet place where we can hear what he is consistently saying. So, what causes Christians to believe that God isn't speaking anymore?

Shortcuts Are Tempting

We all (especially guys) love a good shortcut! As a former resident of Atlanta, it was almost a rite of passage to know all of the ways to avoid traffic jams while navigating the "back ways" of the city… but the truth is, shortcuts can make you lazy! In the beginning of the early church, right after Jesus had risen, the disciples felt that there was a need to fill the vacancy created by the death of Judas Iscariot, and they used the Old Testament practice of "casting lots" to make that decision – the only time this was recorded in the New Testament – with the "lot" falling to a man named Matthias. It's interesting that we never hear anything about Matthias again and, as far as we know, this practice seemed to have been abandoned. The apostles had apparently learned their lesson, but in our modern church culture, it's very tempting to once again "cast lots" by depending on shortcuts to knowing God's will. Here are a few examples:

Shortcut #1: "I Just Follow My Heart"

I've put the most common shortcut first, and it's certainly one that all of us have used at different times. The idea of following your heart takes many forms: some people will say, "I feel a peace about this" while others might say, "There was a stirring in my spirit." At its core, the "I just follow my heart" shortcut depends upon feelings. God created our ability to feel and there are certainly times when we feel things that are both good and bad, but we must never forget the solemn warning about our hearts in Scripture where it says, "The heart is deceitful above all things and beyond cure. Who can understand it?" (Jeremiah 17:9). Notice that the prophet Jeremiah did not say that the heart was bad, but that it was *deceitful*. When something is deceitful, it is influencing you towards thinking one thing, when something else is actually true. A young man might assume that the attraction that he feels to a young woman is God's direction when there is a good chance that it is nothing more than just feelings of physical attraction. A college graduate might have good feelings about a certain career path and assume that God is directing him to take that job, but feelings can be stirred by the prospect of doing a job you like or making a salary that would be acceptable.

Jeremiah made it clear that no one can really "understand" the feelings of the heart, which means that we can enjoy them and sometimes endure them, but we must never use them as a primary way of understanding the will of God. It's not a question of sanctifying your heart until it can be trusted, for Scripture makes it clear that it is "beyond cure" and there is always a danger of deceit when we try to trust our feelings as a shortcut to hearing the voice of God.

The New Testament is so clear on this, it's amazing that we still so often insist on following our feelings and desires. James was pointing to this when he said, "And remember, when you are being tempted, do not say, "'God is tempting me.' God is never tempted to do wrong, and he never tempts anyone else. Temptation comes from our own desires, which entice us and drag us away" (James 1:13-14 NLT). Apparently, what drags us away into directions that God has not called us to is certainly not God, and probably not usually even the devil, it is our own desires which entice us to make decisions that are not based on what God is saying. Again, this doesn't mean that a Christian should fear his emotions or push down his emotions into some kind of pious solemn lifestyle, we should enjoy to the fullest the good desires and the deep passions that God has given us – but we must never let them lead us!

Shortcut #2: "If I'm Wrong God Will Stop Me"

In my opinion, this shortcut is almost a tie for the number one position, for it also is a very common way that Christians make decisions. Very often a person might have a good idea, one that will be of benefit to others and even help build the kingdom of God. He may not know specifically if God has given him that idea but he takes comfort in the fact that, "If I'm wrong, God will stop me." While that sentiment might be true when it comes to babies and toddlers, it seems almost never to be true when it comes to those who God is trying to grow up! The "if I'm wrong God will stop me" shortcut has problems on many levels.

On one level, this shortcut assumes that God's only function is to start and stop us. We forget that Jesus made it clear, God's deepest desire is not to put up guardrails or roadblocks in our lives – it is to lead us! This is what Jesus was talking about when he said, "But when he, the Spirit of truth, comes, he will guide you into all the truth. He will not speak on his own; he will speak only what he hears, and he will tell you what is yet to come" (John 16:13). A guide is not a traffic light or even a map of where you should go – a guide is a companion who goes with you! And anyone who has ever been shown around by a guide in a foreign country knows just what it's like to experience being guided: you have to trust that the guide is taking you to the right place. You also don't need a lot of information about where you're going because you assume that the guide knows where he's going. There is a certain relationship that develops if you spend the day with a guide, you come to know him or her as a person and you receive personal insights beyond just factual information. When we assume that God will stop us if we're wrong, we run the real risk of completely cutting out of our lives the work of the Holy Spirit, whose intention is not to just start or stop us, but to accompany us as a trusted guide who speaks only what he hears from the Father!

On another level, this shortcut is a problem because it ignores the fact that when it comes to good ideas: there is the good and there is the best! I want to quote something Oswald Chambers famously said, "The good is always the enemy of the best."[1] I believe that one day in eternity, we will be very surprised indeed to discover that what kept us from so much of what God had called us to was not our love for the bad, but our willingness to settle for the good! It's comforting to believe that there is a "safety net," where if I inadvertently choose the good over the best, God will eventually stop me, but when it comes to examples we have in the Bible, it's hard to find God actually doing that. When king Saul grew weary of waiting for the prophet Samuel, God didn't stop him from offering sacrifices himself, even though it seemed like a good idea at the time. When Abraham allowed his wife Sarah to substitute her maid in order to fulfill the promise of children in their old age, God didn't stop them even though it opened up a whole new "can of worms" for future history! God loves us and he constantly wants to show us the difference between the good and the best, but we must never assume that we can just do what seems right in our own eyes and expect him to stop us if we are wrong.

Shortcut #3: "I'm Waiting for God to Open the Door"

The real problem with this shortcut is that it is circumstantial in nature: when Christians say, "I'm waiting for the door to open (or shut)," what we mean is that we are waiting for an opportunity to present itself or for some current situation to end. It is true that in the book of Revelation, Jesus said, "I stand at the door and knock" (Rev. 3:20) but in that case, it was the Lord who was waiting for the Laodicean Christians to open the door, not the other way around!

---

[1] Chambers, O. *My Utmost for His Highest.* Retrieved on April 6, 2020, from: https://utmost.org/the-good-or-the-best/

There are many forces in the world that can open and shut doors in our lives, just the act of talking more than praying can oftentimes cause a certain stream of momentum that can be misinterpreted as God's guidance. Years ago, while teaching on this subject, I would use the following illustration about how we can sometimes open our own doors. I would say to the students, "Suppose one morning during my quiet time, I wrote down in my journal that I felt – perhaps – God was calling me to go and live in China. It was only one thought in my mind during prayer and I certainly would need to hear many more words from God, but instead of praying more, suppose I began to talk too much. Later that day I tell a friend of mine that I was surprised to find that – perhaps – God might be calling me to China. He is surprised to hear that news and that evening mentions to his wife that Ralph is feeling a call to China. The next morning she tells her best friend about my call to China who then mentions it to another mutual friend who replies, 'You know there is a Christian school in China that has suddenly lost its director, they could use a guy like Ralph.' Later that day she writes to the school in China who then, one month later, writes me a letter offering me the position. And what do I say? 'Confirmation!' But was it really a confirmation of God's call to China or was it simply a door that opened because I talked more than I prayed?"

In my life as a pastor and teacher in the Philippines, in Russia, and even in America, I've seen God open many doors, but I've learned that the only ones that are safe to walk through are the ones that come after I have clearly and consistently heard from God! We should believe that God can make a way and open or shut doors in our lives and we can rejoice when that happens, but we must never be led by those circumstances!

So, what causes Christians to believe that God isn't speaking anymore?

Hard Hearts Make Us Hard of Hearing

One of the great triumphs that the enemy has won over modern-day Christians is that we no longer understand how all things are connected to each other. This is not only true in a physical sense, but also in all things spiritual. What goes into my eyes has a tremendous influence on what goes on in my mind, and what goes into my stomach can completely alter the energy and vitality that flows out of my life. This connectedness also comes into play when it comes to our ability to hear what God is speaking to us every day. Jesus was pointing to this phenomenon when he said to his disciples, "For this people's heart has become calloused; they hardly hear with their ears, and they have closed their eyes" (Matthew 13:15). It's fascinating to note that Jesus didn't say a hard or callused heart equals a lack of compassion or an inability to have emotion – but an inability to hear with their ears!

Perhaps this truth points to a hidden reason why so many of us struggle in hearing the voice of God: we focus only on our spiritual ears and we don't see the connection between our inability to hear and the condition of our heart! The enemy has done a pretty good job in confusing us over what hardness of heart really means. We have a tendency (when we think of it at all) to equate hardness of heart with "having an evil heart or a rebellious heart." But in the original language of the New Testament, Jesus is using a very specific word that is correctly translated in most versions to read "callused." Anyone who has ever worked with their hands knows full well what calluses are: those hard pads that build up on the places where our hands come into regular contact with the rough handle of a shovel or the unyielding grip of a hammer. We understand what physical calluses are, but what are things that cause us to have a callused heart?

My heart becomes hard when I allow it to embrace the wrong things

Even though our physical hearts are created to be a living pump, circulating blood throughout our body; our spiritual heart has a much different purpose, to love God and to love our neighbor as ourselves. This idea is so important that Jesus actually said that all of religion (all the law and the prophets) hangs on these two things (see Matthew 22:40). And yet, every day we are tempted to apply our hearts to the "rough-textured" things it wasn't really created to embrace. When I give my heart to selfish pleasures, it begins to create a callus as my tender heart comes into constant contact with the coarse texture of rude joking and lewd images. When I give my heart to my career, it begins to toughen as I make cynical decisions in the office and small compromises for the good of the company. God created us to enjoy life's pleasures and to work hard and to build up good things in our society, but our heart was never designed to embrace those things! Only the soft "texture" of the Holy Spirit and the human spirit that lives in our neighbors are non-abrasive enough for our heart to embrace without becoming hard.

My Heart Becomes Hard When I Don't Keep It Stirred

When I was a child, I was always fascinated by big machinery. My father worked in a large construction company that created most of the interstate highway system and many of the new suburbs in the state of Alabama back in the 60s. I always wondered, when I would look at the big concrete trucks backing up to pour sidewalks, why the big drum on the truck that contained the concrete was constantly turning at a slow pace. Only later did I realize that it is only this stirring motion that keeps the concrete from becoming set and hard.

It's not always easy to let things "stir your heart" because when your heart is stirred you feel deep emotions and sometimes deep pain.

It's human nature to want to avoid extreme feelings, but sometimes in our desire to be comfortable we stop stirring our heart and, like that cement in the cement truck, it begins to thicken and can even become as hard as concrete. I've discovered in my life that the best way to stir your heart is not to try to work up emotions in church, but to allow yourself to constantly interact with the people in your city and in your neighborhood. A short dialogue with a homeless person always stirs my heart, as well as a friendly word with a neighbor or a willingness to listen to someone's troubles. We live in a culture today where it's easy to isolate yourself: ordering from Amazon instead of going to the store or working from home and keeping your car in a closed garage. It's all very convenient but it can also, if you are not careful, cause the "big drum" in our hearts to stop rotating, leading eventually to a hard heart.

My Heart Becomes Hard When I Don't Keep A "Shortlist" With God

It's so easy to let the list get long of things I do that I know are wrong, but haven't been brought to God: "I know I should make things right with my wife (and God) concerning that cruel statement I made this morning" or "I know that my eyes weren't looking in the direction they should have been looking last night." But I somehow let the items on my list pile up until those things don't really even feel wrong anymore! The wisest king who ever lived, realized this phenomenon when he wrote, "Whoever conceals his transgressions will not prosper, but he who confesses and forsakes them will obtain mercy. Blessed is the one who fears the Lord always, but whoever hardens his heart will fall into calamity" (Proverbs 28:13-14). When I lose a healthy fear of the Lord and no longer see the need to daily bring things before him, unconfessed sin begins to build a heavy callus around my heart as a result, thickening its spiritual tissue and hardening its ability to operate. It's important to remember that the reason we want to fight against the hardening of our hearts is much greater than just the desire to be emotional in our Christianity, it is for the important reason that the condition of my heart has a direct influence on my ability to hear with my ears!

Not only are there real reasons why people don't believe that God speaks anymore, there are also real consequences to that belief. Let's close this chapter by looking briefly at what happens when I allow myself to be convinced that God isn't really speaking:

Consequence #1: Moldy Bread Will Make You Sick

If Jesus were telling the truth that day when he declared to the enemy in the midst of the wilderness, "Man shall not live by bread alone but by every word that comes from the mouth of God" (Matthew 4:4), then the obvious conclusion is that if I am not hearing words that come from the mouth of God and depend solely on words coming from someone else's mouth, then I am trying to live on a diet of moldy bread!

When my wife and I returned from Russia in 2009, God gave me a strange mental image one morning in my quiet time: I saw a concentration camp survivor, emaciated and skinny beyond belief, with a sunken face and staring eyes. I went online and found a similar image from the concentration camps in Germany and one Sunday, when it was my turn to preach, I projected the image for the church and prefaced it by saying rather prophetically, "This is what God sees when he looks at his church in America!" I'm not sure that this statement from the newly returned missionary, now associate pastor, was greatly appreciated that morning, but I have always believed that it was a true image of 21st-century Christianity. So many believers today have so little time in their lives that they are lucky to get enough physical bread, much less be nourished by every word that comes from the mouth of God. There is a deadly downward spiral that happens in many believer's lives where they get just enough nourishment on Sunday to make it through the week but return to the next service a little weaker. Then, the following service, they become even weaker still, until many reach a point where the spiritual man or woman is close to the edge of spiritual death! In trying to understand what is happening, people so often believe that there must be some hidden sin in their lives, or perhaps God has lost interest in them – when the truth is simple: they are starving! The true consequence of not consistently hearing what God is saying is much greater than just not knowing what to do at times; it is a question of spiritual life and death. Later in the book, we will talk about this important role that taking dictation plays in our growth as Christians, but for now, we must never forget that when we don't eat, there are always consequences.

Consequence #2: Following Becomes Only Believing

After coming to Christ as young "hippies" in Northern California in 1976, many of us didn't like to refer to ourselves as "Christians" so we would tell people, "I am a follower of Jesus." But later in my life, I began to wonder just what exactly I meant when I said that I was a follower of Jesus. Did it just mean that I tried to only follow his teachings? But I knew by then that my Christian life was not a set of religious rules I tried to follow every day, but a relationship. Did following Jesus mean that I was only trying to act like him? Around that time there was a popular book, *What Would Jesus Do?* complete with plastic bracelets that had WWJD stamped into the plastic. But after a while, we discovered that it's very difficult to try and anticipate what Jesus might do in every situation, and in attempting to do so, we would often end up creating a kind of Jesus-in-your-own-image. It took me a little while, but I finally came to realize that following Jesus means – actually following him! And to follow him you have to have a way of knowing just where he is going and where he is leading you.

When we don't believe that God is really speaking anymore, we oftentimes become somewhat hypocritical in our relationship with Jesus (without realizing it). We say that we are followers but we often don't really have a very good answer if we are asked, "Where is he leading you?" The result is a kind of "following" which is really just doing what seems best to me or what someone else thinks that Jesus might be speaking to me. The term "following" simply becomes another way to say I believe that Jesus exists, or I agree that what the Bible says about him is true.

Consequence #3: Relationship Is No Longer a Reality

As a pastor who has struggled through many marital counseling sessions with couples, I know, without a doubt, that relationships die when there is no communication! It doesn't matter how compatible a couple might be, or how attracted they may have been to each other in the beginning, if they are only talking at each other and not listening to each other, the relationship will suffer.

I've always found it fascinating that when the apostle Paul was talking about marriage, he pointed out that it is an illustration of something much greater than just companionship or family. He said, "As the Scriptures say, 'a man leaves his father and mother and is joined to his wife, and the two are united into one.' This is a great mystery, but it is an illustration of the way that Christ and the church are "one" (Ephesians 5:31-32 NLT). It's easy to read those words and miss a very important concept: the relationship between Christ and his church is supposed to have the same dynamics as the relationship between a man and his wife! Many Christians diligently work on being good communicators in their marriages, but so often fail to see that the same dynamic applies to their relationship with God. In the end, God's greatest desire is not just to direct us but to reconcile us and draw us deeply into his family. The core motivation behind everything he does in our lives is to draw us deeper into a relationship with him, and when we stop communicating, that relationship shrivels. We will return to several of these important concepts later in the book, but for now, it's crucial that we realize not only what causes us to no longer hear the voice of God, but also what the inevitable consequences are when we stop believing that he speaks.

Questions to Ponder

1. How does your life sometimes resemble a crowded room? What are some of the things in your daily life that drown out the still small voice of God?

2. Have you been tempted to take shortcuts in discerning the will of God for your life? What are the dangers of things like following your heart, or believing that God will stop you if you're wrong, or even waiting for a certain door to open?

3. Have you found there are times in your life when the hardness of your heart has had an indirect effect on the openness of your hearing? Can you give some examples of how these two things are connected?

4. If human beings cannot live by bread alone, what are the consequences when you ignore the nourishment of every word that comes from the mouth of God?

5. If we are followers of Jesus, what are the consequences if we are unable to hear his direction?

Chapter Two

Three Reasons Why God Chooses to Speak

One of the most unusual things about the one true God that we serve is that his most distinguishing characteristic is not his power or his omnipotence… but the fact that he is the God who speaks! From almost the moment he is introduced in the book of Genesis, we are told, in the third verse of the very first chapter, "And God said…" (Genesis 1:3). While some people might see the book of Genesis as an allegorical and not a purely literal account of the creation of the world, it is still very important that we understand that *God used words* to create everything that is around us. He said, "Let there be light," and he said, "Let dry ground appear," and he said, "Let the land produce vegetation," and he said, "Let the water team with living creatures, and let birds fly above the earth" (see Genesis 1). I believe that it's very important we think about *why* God chose to use words when he spoke the universe into being, he could have just snapped his fingers (like Thanos in *The Avengers*) if he had chosen to, but instead, he deliberately chose to speak!

Although the fall of man has darkened God's creation, we can still see in the way that we are created, how powerful and important words really are. In one of the most surprising (and troubling) passages in the New Testament, James had this to say about the power of words, "We all stumble in many ways. Anyone who is never at fault in what they say is perfect, able to keep their whole body in check. When we put bits into the mouths of horses to make them obey us, we can turn the whole animal. Or take ships as an example. Although they are so large and are driven by strong winds, they are steered by a very small rudder wherever the pilot wants to go. Likewise, the tongue is a small part of the body, but it makes great boasts. Consider what a great forest is set on fire by a small spark" (James 3:2-5). If human words have the power to steer the direction of our lives in much the same way as a bit and bridle directs a powerful horse or a rudder steers a huge freighter, how much greater is the spoken word of God able to steer our lives! If human words are able to provide a spark that can cause a great forest fire, what kind of holy fire is God able to create in our lives with a single word? God has given that much power and authority to words spoken by human beings because it is meant to be an illustration of the power and the authority of every word that comes from his mouth!

It's important to remember when we come to God, that we can't come to some picture of what we would like him to be: an empowering force or a kindly presence. We must come to God as he is presented in the Bible: one who has sovereignly *chosen to use words* in his creation of mankind and in his dealings with their descendants. The real question is not, "Does God speak?" but, "Why does he choose to speak to us?"

Perhaps the most basic answer to that question is found in the kind of relationship God has chosen to have with human beings. We sometimes confuse the process of Christ's work on the cross with what was meant to be the result. The death of Jesus on the cross, paying the penalty for our sin, might be the process, but the whole point of it all is expressed in II Corinthians where it says, "God was reconciling the world to himself in Christ, not counting people's sins against them" (II Corinthians 5:19). Jesus went through the suffering of the cross not just to provide a convenient target for the wrath of God, but to fulfill the deepest desire that God has towards us: that we be reconciled to him! The word "reconciliation" means that differences are laid down and there is a restoration of the relationship we had before things went wrong. We only have to look at the record of that original relationship with Adam and Eve to understand that it was one of intimacy and communication. So, the basic answer to the question, "Why does God choose to speak to us?" is answered when we understand God's motivation for our salvation: not just to fix us or improve our lives, but to restore us into the family of God.

While this is true, in order to become a person truly committed to hearing the voice of God, we need a more specific reason than just, "God speaks because he wants to." To put it in terms of the world, to really commit myself to something I need to see what the benefit is for me. The following three reasons why God chooses to speak should be enough to awaken in any heart a deep hunger to start listening.

#1: God Chooses to Speak Because He Wants His Children to Know His Specific Will

Somehow, in our modern church culture, we've gotten the idea that God only has a kind of "general will" towards the human race. Christians assume that God only wants us to be as good as we can be and to love him and others with all of our heart – with the rest being pretty much up to us – but when you look at the record that we have of God in the Bible, you realize that nothing could be further from the truth!

When giving Noah instructions on how to construct the ark, God didn't just say, "Build a big boat." Instead, he gave detailed instructions as to its length and width and even the type of wood and pitch that should be used. God had a very specific will for Abraham when he told him to leave his father and mother and go to a country he did not know. God wouldn't allow Moses to use his influence as a prince to deliver his people but had a very specific way that he wanted to do it, a way that Moses never seemed terribly comfortable with. And when Moses led his people through the wilderness, the portable house of God that they carried was constructed in the greatest detail, according to the specific will of God.

When you read your Bible, you cannot deny that God is interested in communicating in great detail not only what he wants us to do, but also how he feels about us. One way that the enemy has countered this is to (as he always does) present us with a distorted picture of what this looks like. Most of us have met the "over-prophetic" type of Christian who enjoys fixing you with a prophetic eye and declaring, "Thus saith the Lord" to the great discomfort of the receiver. None of us wants to be that guy, so we tend to – as we say in Alabama – throw out the baby with the bathwater! We become content with the general will of God and no longer really believe that he wants to direct the specific details of our lives. But if we really are his sheep and if he really is our shepherd, how in the world can we operate in life if we don't know the day-to-day will of the one who is guiding us? Jesus made it clear that the title "shepherd" was not just honorary when he said, "My sheep listen to my voice; I know them, and they follow me. I give them eternal life, and they shall never perish; no one will snatch them out of my hand" (John 10:27-28). Notice that the sheep in this statement do not follow the shepherd by being started or stopped by the staff of the shepherd, but through having the ability to listen to his voice! It seems that, more than in any other profession, shepherds are intimately involved with their charges. They are with the sheep day and night and it is they who decide where the sheep will eat and drink and lay down to sleep. Their safety depends on their intimate knowledge of the shepherd and their ability to hear his specific direction as they listen to his voice.

In 1998, when my wife and I, along with our infant son, moved to Perm, Russia, there was a lot of pressure to start a church as quickly as possible. Many people in those days believed that Russia would not be open for very long, and it was fairly logical to try to establish something in a short time before the doors closed and all the foreigners were kicked out. We had come into Russia that year with a team from our church, and after doing evangelism throughout the city, it was bittersweet the day that we put them on the train to Moscow and watched the train pull away from the station – without us! As the train dwindled in the distance, we turned to the family who had chosen to stay with us and said to each other, "So what exactly do we do now?" The answer that we heard from God in our prayer journal was just the opposite of what you would expect church planters in Russia to do: God said we were *not* to gather people or do anything else church-related for the first year! Instead, we were to study the Russian language and, most importantly, to pray over the city of Perm. Thus began a wonderful year of praying in almost every way that we had ever heard of: we made a prayer map of the city and traveled to the highest point and prayed, as well as the lowest point. We visited the local universities and sat in the school cafeteria and prayed; we walked the streets of the city and prayed and gathered almost every day in our small apartment to seek the specific will of God. By the end of that first year, we knew a lot more than just God's general will to plant a church in Perm, Russia; we knew that God had called us to the industrial region of that city and that God fully intended to create a missionary-minded church which would, even in its early stages, reproduce itself into other cities.

We had a pretty specific vision of how God wanted to build his church and we spent the next ten years building it. As of this writing, that church is now twenty years old, and despite the challenges, it continues not only to exist but to grow as the body of Christ in Perm, Russia. I understand that whatever success that work has had, it wasn't down to my skill as a church planter, it was because we chose to believe that God wanted us to know his specific will on how to start his church through loving acts of service!

The very fact that God chose to reveal himself not through the Ten Commandments only, but to become flesh and dwell among us, should be a clear indication that he is very interested in the details! The disciples didn't just meet Jesus once a day on a mountaintop, they lived with him. They learned in great detail what he liked and what he didn't like and by the time they were ready to go on without him, he sent his promised Holy Spirit to continue to lead them in great detail.

It is true that God has given us a mind and a will and that he wants us to use it, but we must never forget that whatever God gives us becomes much more useful if we are willing to first lay it on the altar as a living sacrifice and then receive it back in a way that is empowered and transformed by his presence. There's an old saying that says, "the devil is in the details," which means, I suppose, that the problem with great vision is working out the details of that vision, but I believe that just the opposite is a greater truth: "God is always dictating the details." If we really want to fulfill the vision that he has given us, we must set our minds to the task of learning his specific will.

#2: God Chooses to Speak Because He Wants Healthy Children

I want to return now to the idea first presented in chapter one, the fact that moldy bread will make you sick. So often, we think about prayer journals only in the context of finding out the will of God or receiving specific direction in our lives, but there is a much more important reason why God chooses to speak: if his words are not flowing into our hearts we will become malnourished and unhealthy. When Jesus was tempted in the wilderness to turn stones into bread, his reply to the enemy was one of the most important principles a

Christian can learn in his life: the fact that physical bread alone will not bring spiritual life! And it is significant that Jesus didn't say that life comes from every word written in the Torah, but every word that comes from the mouth of God (see Matthew 4:4).

In my seven years of pastoring Americans in the city of Atlanta, I became convinced that this was one of the great "missing ingredients" in discipling Christians. The spiritual weakness and lack of development that a pastor encounters so often have nothing to do with the education or the sophistication of his congregation. In the 1980s, I met tribal Christians who had an amazing maturity even though they had little or no education. What seems to stunt Christian growth is simply the Christian's unwillingness to find nourishment every day from every word that comes from the mouth of God.

A couple of years into my role as a pastor in Atlanta, I started mentoring people in the art of spending consistent time with God and writing down in a journal their impressions of what he might be saying. As the years went by, I noticed a very interesting pattern: not only would people begin to have a greater sense of God's specific will for their lives, but I also noticed that they began to grow significantly in their spiritual health. That growth had several important characteristics...

Healthy Children Change Rapidly

You only have to visit a niece or nephew after a long absence to appreciate the fact that healthy children grow almost before your eyes! The short skinny boy you knew last year is now a tall young man. I discovered that, almost without exception, when people began to really feed on every word that comes from the mouth of God, they rapidly began to change into mature Christians.

One of my early "mentorees" was a middle-aged man who had had a successful career in engineering, but unfortunately, he made several bad decisions that eventually caused him to be imprisoned for several years. When I met him, he was newly released from prison and still had an ankle monitor on one foot, so we laid down some ground rules and invited him to join our church family. When I first began meeting with him, he had many strong ideas that had developed during his years of forced isolation in a prison cell, but as he began to journal, he began to radically change. One of the ways that I mentor people is to ask them to meet with me on a weekly basis and read to me from their prayer journal. As he began to read day after day to me, I saw a beautiful change take place in this man: the loving words of his Heavenly Father started to heal the many wounds he had received from his earthly parents, and very gently and lovingly God brought him to a place of authentic humility and servanthood. Today he leads a ministry to the homeless and the needy in our city that is slowly starting to transform hopeless people into disciples of Jesus. Going from an inmate in a federal prison to the leader of a ministry for the poor in just seven years is what I would call rapid change!

Healthy Children have a Father's Love and Approval

Although I am certainly no psychologist, I think that all psychologists would agree that a father's approval is one of the most crucial aspects in the psychological development of children. There is a very core and very basic human need for the blessing of a father. Sometimes when I talk with people about journaling, I can tell from their questions that they see what I do as primarily a way to get information in order to lead the church or to make decisions as a pastor; but the truth is that most of the contents of my journal are not detailed directions, but the encouraging words of a father to a son who daily needs to hear them!

Because the need for approval is such a basic need for all human beings, there is a tendency for us to try to find approval in other ways when we cease to believe that God wants to speak anymore. It might be the approval from others that comes from success in our careers, or the approval we seek from a wife or a husband, but we cannot ignore the fact that seeking approval in the wrong way will always lead to the wrong results. I read not long ago that the real reason why people in the West live such frantically busy lifestyles is the simple reason that if they are busy they feel as though life is important and has meaning, but so often the approval of society has a terrible cost: isolation from family and a life that is slowly consumed by work and advancement.

Even Jesus, that living paradox who was 100% God and yet also 100% man, had many times in his life where he needed more than just direction from his Heavenly Father. I believe it is significant that at the very beginning of the ministry of Jesus, when he came up out of the water after having allowed John to baptize him, the first thing that God declared from heaven was, "This is my son, whom I love; with him I am well pleased" (Matthew 3:17). Most of my life I've always read that statement as something being said to the crowd, but I believe it was also an important word for Jesus the Son! As a pastor, I've seen firsthand how many people have deep wounds that have been inflicted by either their fathers or authority figures in their lives, and one thing I've learned is that time never heals those wounds! Only the healing touch of a heavenly father can begin to reverse the wounding touch of an earthly father. If my father has rejected me, I need a father's acceptance in order to be healed. If my father has betrayed me, I need a father's faithfulness to reverse that failure. If my father has abused me, I need a father's loving touch to unwind the terrible effects of that abuse. Counseling and psychological techniques are very important in the healing process, but I also firmly believe that there are certain things that only a Father can do when it comes to healing, and that he chooses to use words, spoken to our hearts from the pages of our journal to accomplish that healing.

Healthy Children Don't Burn Out

The term "burnout" is one that is used fairly commonly in Christian culture. It usually refers to a visionary pastor or an overzealous volunteer who gets so involved in ministry that they use up all of their resources and quickly run out of gas in a few years. Even though that certainly happens in many churches, I don't think we understand at all the reason why it happens, or the solution when it does.

One of the great characteristics of healthy children is that they have a seemingly unlimited store of energy! Every parent wonders how in the world that little 35-pound package is able to go at such a rate every day! There is great energy in the life of a child and the source of that energy is not just biological, but also situational. A healthy child in a healthy environment is surrounded by a loving, nurturing environment which provides an abundance of strength and joy and energy.

It's no coincidence that Jesus said to his disciples, "Unless you change and become like little children, you will never enter the kingdom of heaven" (Matthew 18:3). I've always been a bit confused by that statement, because we know that entering the kingdom of heaven is not accomplished by changing oneself in any way. Perhaps Jesus meant that the energy we need in order to enter into the work of the kingdom of heaven and to be fully functioning kingdom people requires a healthy child of the Father that has no fear of burnout!

In 40 years of trying to obey the Lord in things that have raised a few eyebrows – living with the poor in the Philippines in my 30s, learning Russian in my 40s, and moving to India in my mid-60s – I have made the happy discovery that burnout never has to happen! If I live daily by every word that proceeds from the mouth of the Father, and not by bread alone, then I have all of the nourishment and energy that I need to do anything that God calls me to do. God chooses to speak because he has chosen us to be physically and mentally healthy and never stop growing and transforming into the image of his Son!

#3: God Chooses To Speak Because He Wants Confident Children

We have all seen (and even experienced) the effects that a lack of confidence has on the development of a human life: without confidence, it's easy to slip into the back of the crowd at church and never find your place of service. Without confidence, it's very difficult to say, "Yes Lord" when God begins to show you things much greater than yourself.

Many people make the false assumption that the degree of confidence one has in one's life is completely dependent on the amount of natural talent or giftings one happens to have. It becomes easy to justify a lack of confidence by thinking, "Well, I'm just not that kind of person" and embracing a mediocre life, instead of the full and fruitful life that God means them to have. God needs a people who not only have confidence in him, but also the kingdom of God and each other. His solution does not just pour confidence into us or to overwhelm our will by making us feel more confident, as we so often hope for; his solution involves speaking to us! Let's look at three examples of how his choice to speak creates the confidence that we need as kingdom people.

Confidence Comes When You Are Part of Something Bigger Than Yourself

A traffic cop is able to step into the flow of live traffic, hold up his hand, and have confidence that the motorists will stop; not because he has confidence in his own physical ability to stop moving cars, but simply because he knows that he is part of something bigger than himself – the police force. He joined that force and went through intensive training to be on that force. He's learned the laws that he enforces as a policeman and all of those things work together to give him the confidence to step in front of a moving car!

Most Christians have a theoretical knowledge of the fact that they are part of something bigger than themselves, namely the kingdom of God. But for most of us, that is not enough. I can have a theoretical understanding of the police force but that alone will not give me the confidence (or the authority) to direct traffic, I need a deeper knowledge than just theoretical knowledge.

In the book of Hebrews, there's an interesting sequence that is sometimes easy to overlook because it's in the middle of a lot of practical advice about hospitality and marriage and other things. In the 13th chapter, it says, "Keep your lives free from the love of money and be content with what you have, because God has said, never will I leave you; never will I forsake you. So, we say with confidence, The Lord is my helper; I will not be afraid. What can mere mortals do to me?" (Hebrews 13:5-6). Did you hear the sequence? "Because God has said – so we say with confidence!" There is a direct link in that verse between hearing what God is saying and being able to then say things myself with confidence.

A few years into our attempt to establish a church in Perm, Russia, it became clear to me that there was a much greater need in the nation than just the needs of my small local church. At that time, there were about half a dozen church plants scattered around the nation but all of them desperately needed Russian pastors. For many months God had been speaking to me in my journal about starting a pastor's school that would draw young Russian leaders from around the country. The vision that God gave me was not just of a Bible school or correspondence school, but a live-in community where students would study together twenty-four-seven, and after eight months of intensive lectures would have three months of internship in local churches. As I began to pull together how such a school like that might cost and sketch out the kind of training I felt young pastors needed, I realized that there was one big missing ingredient – I wasn't at all confident that I could pull it off! I was a full-time pastor and the only staff I had for the school was my faithful spiritual daughter who had been my sermon translator for several years. Although we would charge students tuition, it would not come close to the costs involved in renting an entire floor of a Russian hotel on the outskirts of the city. Although there are people in the world that have great confidence in their own ability to raise money and pull resources together, I certainly wasn't one of them. However, to remind myself of what God had said, I began to go back over dozens of journal entries where God had carefully laid down the vision for the school, and I was then able to confidently say, "The Lord is my helper, I will not be afraid."

Looking back, I'm convinced that the only way I was able to pull together such a big and complicated vision was simply because God's word showed me that I was part of something much bigger than myself. As God showed me the details of what the school would look like and emphasized the community and discipleship elements of the school, I became more and more convinced that this wasn't just some good idea from Ralph, but a school that had the backing of the kingdom of heaven. There were still many times when we had to "pray in" the rent and to trust God for the right speakers, but it was a confident time of seeing God meet our needs every month for 11 months – and at the end of that time, we had new Russian pastors in two different cities as well as two missionaries taking part in the planting of a church in the Muslim nation of Tajikistan!

Confidence Comes When You Already Know What God Has Said

Anyone who has ever spoken in public knows that your confidence level is always directly connected to your level of preparation. I am by nature an introvert who doesn't do well before people if I'm speaking off-the-cuff, but if I already know what I want to say and I've crafted the words and sought the mind of God, then I find that I can be a confident introvert no matter who invites me to come and speak! My favorite Old Testament character is Moses – not the Charlton Heston Moses of the movies, but Moses the introvert whom the Bible called "meeker than any man on the face of the earth" (Numbers 12:3). He definitely didn't have the confidence to do the job that God had called him to, he even turned over a lot of the speaking parts to his brother Aaron, but he was able to stand with confidence before Pharaoh, the mightiest king on Earth, and demand his people's freedom because God had already told him – in great detail – what he intended to do! The night before every confrontation with Pharaoh, God spoke and told Moses exactly what the next level of plagues would look like. He wasn't standing before the court of Pharaoh and just hoping something would come to him, he had the confidence of knowing what God had already said!

If you think about it, this confidence was the great hidden key to really understanding how a man like Moses could have led his people out of slavery and then towards the promised land through the wilderness, on a path that was so circuitous that everyone, including his closest friends, had second thoughts about his leadership – and the source of his confidence was how regularly God spoke to him! God spoke to Moses so often that they set up a special tent for that purpose a little outside the camp, calling it "The Tent of Meeting." God spoke to Moses so intently that it actually caused physical changes in his body: his face shining to the degree that the people asked him to cover it with a veil. There is one verse in the book of Exodus that really sums up this great key to the confidence of Moses, "The Lord would speak to Moses face to face, as one speaks to a friend" (Exodus 33:11). Confidence doesn't come only through seeing God's power or his wrath over his enemies, the confidence to lead an entire nation out of slavery was only developed through an intimacy in communication, face-to-face, in the relationship of a friend to a friend!

I sometimes feel rather embarrassed when people express wonder over our confidence to take our one-year-old son and move to Russia in our early 40s, or to leave the church that we were pastoring to take up residence in India in our mid-60s. I'm embarrassed because I know that Vicki and I are not particularly brave people, we just have dozens of entries in our journal – our tent of meeting – where God has met with us face-to-face as a friend meets with his friend and shown us what he wanted us to do. I know without a doubt, that I could have never gotten on the plane to Perm, Russia, or Visakhapatnam, India, if I had not had a good deal of evidence of what God had already said.

Confidence Is an Expression Of Faith

When the writer of Hebrews said, "Now faith is confidence in what we hope for and assurance about what we do not see" (Hebrews 11:1), the author was drawing an indelible line between faith and confidence. Almost every believer knows this verse, but we so often don't think about what it's really saying. It's describing faith as being confident and assured about something that is only a hope and that we do not see. How does a person develop confidence and assurance over something as intangible and invisible as something we hope for? I believe there can be only one answer: Faith is developed not by focusing on how confident you are (that only leads to a "name it and claim it" kind of hyper faith). It is developed when I have an assurance of what God is saying to me. There is strong evidence for this found in other places in the New Testament. Paul in the book of Romans put it this way, *"So then faith comes by hearing, and hearing by the word of God"* (Romans 10:17 NKJ). This is a verse that God has taken me back to many times in my Christian life; faith doesn't come through psyching up oneself or building up emotions or even through knowledge and experience – it comes through hearing the word of God!

As a pastor, I am constantly amazed that people don't see this connection between the maturity of their faith in God and their willingness to hear the words of God. I believe that it is significant that Paul didn't say faith comes by studying the Scriptures but by hearing God's words. Many people expect their faith to grow simply because they study the Bible, not realizing that the Bible operates in two distinct ways in their lives. In the Greek, Scripture is sometimes described as "logos" which means a teaching or a form of instruction. We need this operation of the word of God in our lives. It is also described in the Greek as "rhema" which means a specific word from the Bible to our hearts. We will see later in the book that learning to make the transition from *logos* to *rhema* is an important first step in journaling, but for now, we must see that hearing the word is also an indispensable step to having authentic faith!

I'm sometimes asked, "How did you have the faith to move to India at a time of life when most people your age are settling into their retirement years?" My answer, at first, sounds very spiritual, "I have confidence that God is calling us there." But when pressed about how I could be so confident, my next statement is rather an anticlimax, "I'm confident of the things I'm hoping for in India simply because, for five years while pastoring in the city of Atlanta, God spoke again and again and many times again in my prayer journal." I've never really had a vision from God or very many significant dreams in the night; I've never had an angelic visitation or anything very dramatic happen in my relationship with God, but I can say with a straight face that God speaks to me almost every day – it is those words, not the dramatic stuff, that are the foundation of my faith!

No one who has had any exposure to the Bible can deny that God is one who speaks, but we miss so much that is important to our growth if we don't understand why he has chosen to speak. He chooses to speak because we are not just a machine that he winds up and releases, we are children who need to know his specific will for our lives. He chooses to speak because he understands that Christian growth is much more than just information, it only occurs when we learn to receive nourishment from every word that proceeds from the mouth of God. He chooses to speak because he needs a confident people willing to say in faith, "Yes, Lord" when he calls us to go out and change the world!

Questions to Ponder

1. What does the fact that God used words to create the universe tell you about the power of words? What does it also tell you about the importance of words to God?

2. Why are words important in the process of being reconciled into the family of God?

3. If God chooses to speak sin order that you might know his specific will, how does that change the way you make decisions?

4. If God chooses to speak because he wants healthy children, how does this change your understanding of spiritual health and maturity?

5. If God chooses to speak because he wants confident followers, how does this redefine how confidence is developed in your life?

Chapter Three

God's Voice in His Word

The Bible, which Christians commonly call "the Word of God," plays a wide variety of roles in the lives of Christians. For some, it has an honored place on the bookshelf, but doesn't occupy much space in their daily lives. To others, it's seen as a source for inspiring and uplifting words, not much different than a favorite book of poetry or the favorite lyric of a song. Even the phrase, "the Word of God" is interpreted in many different ways by many different believers. For some, it's seen as only words about God; to others, an infallible truth that covers every topic. But if we are going to learn to hear his voice we must accept (somewhat by faith) that God really has spoken to individuals over the centuries and those words have been preserved in the Bible.

This was certainly the position of the apostle Paul and the other leaders of the first-century church. As Paul said to his young protégé Timothy, "All Scripture is breathed out by God and profitable for teaching, for reproof, for correction, and for training in righteousness, that the man of God may be complete, equipped for every good work" (II Timothy 3:16-17 ESV). The word "Scripture" is a fairly generic word in the Greek, *graphe*, which simply means "writings"; but it was clear in the way Jesus used it in his teaching that he was referring to the holy writings of the Old Testament Scripture. And it's surprising how often he talked about Scripture. At the beginning of his ministry, after reading from the scroll of Isaiah, he declared, "Today this Scripture is fulfilled in your hearing" (Luke 4:21). At the end of his life, it says that the risen Lord, "...[he] explained to them all the things in the Scriptures concerning himself" (Luke 24:27). And even when rebuking his critics, he referred to the power of Scripture in representing the voice of God. When countering the arguments of the Pharisees he said, "Are you not in error because you do not know the Scriptures or the power of God?" (Mark 12:24).

In using the same word "Scripture" Paul makes an important point to his protégé and to all of us in 2 Timothy, all Scripture has this characteristic of being "breathed out." Notice that he didn't say all Scripture comes from the mind of God, but there is this picture of Scripture operating like words issuing from the mouth of God. That doesn't mean that throughout the ages every person has totally understood what God was saying, nor that the culture of the time did not have an influence on how people interpreted what they were hearing from God, but the meaning is clear: the Bible really is the voice of God that was heard by men and women and written down in the pages of a book. The reason why this point is so important is **not** that we should use the Bible as the last word in science or politics or history, but that we realize in learning to hear the voice of God, our starting point must always be the Bible, the Word of God!

If you think about it, the process of learning to recognize someone else's voice is something we've understood since childhood. When I was a child back in the 60s, we lived in neighborhoods filled with families, and in the summertime, we spent most of our day outdoors in each other's yards. When it was time to come in, our mothers would step out of the door and call our names and I remember there was never any confusion over whose mother was calling whom! We all had developed the ability to recognize our mother's voice – even shouted across the neighborhood! It's the same process of repetition and intimacy that develops our ability to recognize a best friend's voice over the telephone, even if it's been years since we've spoken to them. The principle is: spending time communicating with another person attunes our ears to their voice. This tuning process not only allows us to recognize their voice, but can also be fine-tuned to hear when there's something wrong or there's some note of trouble in their voice.

When it comes to our relationship with God, we sometimes forget that many relationship principles between human beings also apply to our relationship with him. Even though he is eternal, he is a "being" in the sense that he thinks and feels and has duplicated in us many of the things that are in his image. I have come to firmly believe that tuning our ears to hear the voice of God works in much the same way as tuning my ear to hear the voice of my mother on a hot summer day. He's not shouting across the neighborhood, but he does shout across the centuries in his Holy Word! It's important that you don't get the impression that I'm simply saying "read your Bible" – for I've discovered that I'm capable of reading God's word and studying God's word and even preaching God's word – without necessarily hearing God's voice in his word for me! Let's look at three principles for hearing God's voice in God's word.

Principle #1 To Hear God's Voice in His Word We Must Read His Word

In any relationship, people understand that to learn to really hear each other you have to take the time to talk and listen to each other. I can never grow in my ability to hear my wife if she never speaks to me! And yet we somehow expect to grow in hearing God's Word, even though we spend little or no time listening to God speak through his word! We become very dependent on secondhand accounts of what God is saying through books or sermons, but we don't spend much time directly soaking in God's Word.

I'm often asked, "How much of the Bible should I be reading?" And even though I think it's good to have a schedule for reading through the Word (two chapters in the Old Testament and one chapter in the New Testament will get you through the Bible in a year) the more important question is not how much should I be reading, but *how well am I listening?*

Bible reading can become a rather dry endeavor if I'm really not taking in what the word is trying to give to me. The writer of the book of Hebrews gives us a very good rule of thumb in determining how well I am listening, "For the word of God is alive and active. Sharper than any double-edged sword, it penetrates even to dividing soul and spirit, joints and marrow; it judges the thoughts and attitudes of the heart." (Hebrews 4:12). Notice that this verse is not really talking about what the Word of God is, but what it *does* when we are really listening. What's important to God is not how much we are studying or questioning his word, but how much we're allowing his word to question us. According to this verse, how can I know if I'm reading enough of God's word?

I'm Reading Enough If It's Influencing My Life

When the Bible says the word is "alive and active" it's obviously not saying that the printed words in the book themselves are moving around the page, but that they begin to move around within our lives when we really listen to them. I believe there's something a little deceptive in just disciplining oneself to read so many chapters each day in a personal quiet time. Mere quantity doesn't guarantee that the word is alive and active in my life, that comes only when it's influencing my behavior!

I'm Reading Enough If It's Dividing Soul and Spirit

I've always found this illustration (which sounds like it comes straight out of a butcher shop) to be very intriguing. The Word of God is "sharper than any two-edged sword" and, just as a butcher's sharp blade can divide joints and marrow, the Word of God divides soul and spirit. In the Greek, these are two words that usually describe two unseen aspects of the breath of life: the soul *(psyke)* is the seat of all feelings, desires, and affections, and the spirit *(pneuma)* is the eternal spirit of man formed in the image of God's Holy Spirit. And even though both words can seem rather interchangeable, it is significant that the writer of Hebrews believed it was important to divide them from one another in our understanding. As I mentioned in the first chapter, it's easy to fall into the bad, soulish, habit of substituting feelings as a way of following God's will or deciding on some good idea with the false hope that God will stop me if I'm wrong. It's amazing how the Word of God has the ability to help us see what's coming from just the *psyke*, our feelings and desires and affections, and what is being influenced by the *pneuma*, the part of self that is yielded to the *pneuma* of God. Treating a great church leader in the same way that we would treat a great world leader might seem like a good and honoring idea, but the Word of God shows us the category that idea is really in when it tells us that the greatest among you should be like a servant. There might be a certain logic to the good idea that we are all king's kids and that we should be materially prosperous as part of our witness to the world, but that gets divided pretty quickly by the words of Jesus who said, "It is hard for someone who is rich to enter the Kingdom of Heaven" (Matthew 19:23). If I'm reading enough of God's word, I can tell pretty easily if I am automatically letting it illuminate what ideas are soulish and what ideas are spiritual in the course of my day.

I'm Reading Enough If It's Judging My Heart

When the writer of Hebrews talks about the Word of God "judging the thoughts and the intents of my heart," this isn't only in the sense of judging sinful desires and affections (although it certainly can do that) but also in the sense of helping us see the motives and the true aims of our heart. When Mr. Spock, the Vulcan second-in-command in the old TV series *Star Trek*, would say, "Emotions are not logical," he was actually speaking something very true about the nature of human beings — that our heart can have secret motives that are hidden from our mind and can direct our lives into places we would not logically choose to go! The Word of God has an amazing ability to shine light on not only what I'm feeling, but also why I am feeling it.

Growing up in the great state of Alabama in the 1960s my heart was filled with the racism that was rampant at the time. Even though my parents were good people, and I considered myself to be a kind person, it wasn't until I came to Christ and began to let the Word divide things that the true thoughts and attitudes of my heart were revealed. If I had been content to settle for an inspiring verse every now and then, I'm not sure that I would have said yes to God's call to people of color in the Philippines or to his command to pastor a multi-ethnic church in Atlanta. Looking back, I know that I was reading enough of God's Word because of how much God's Word revealed to me concerning the motives of my own heart.

While it is very true that to hear God's voice in his Word you have to read his Word on a consistent basis, it's also true that reading his Word consistently does not guarantee that you will hear his voice. If you are willing to let his Word influence you and divide the soulish from the spiritual and reveal the motives of your heart, then whether you're reading one verse a day or ten chapters a day, you are probably reading enough!

Principle #2: To Hear God's Voice in His Word We Must Digest God's Word

To really develop the skill of hearing God's voice in his Word, we must understand that not only is God's Word information, it is also nourishment! We saw this earlier when Jesus responded to the devil's temptation to turn stones into bread by saying, "Man shall not live by bread alone, but by every word that proceeds from the mouth of God" (Matthew 4:4) and now we want to return to this idea of God's Word being spiritual food and apply it to tuning our ears to God's voice.

While it is true that most people have the ability to eat a ten-ounce steak, there is no one who can swallow that steak in one bite! And even if one could, it would lead to a whole host of gastronomic problems later. Obviously, you have to cut that steak into bite-size pieces, then chew each piece into even smaller pieces, and digest them in your stomach into even smaller pieces before that ten-ounce steak will ever be good for you.

In his letter to his young protégé Timothy, Paul seemed to be pointing to this idea when he said, "Be diligent to present yourself approved to God, a worker who does not need to be ashamed, rightly dividing the word of truth." (II Timothy 2:15 NKJ) A lot of newer translations, in my opinion, miss the whole point when they translate that part of the sentence to read, *"Correctly handling the word of truth."* In the Greek, it's a very specific and common word, *orthotomeō*, which means "to make a straight cut." And that, in truth, is the only way you can correctly handle God's Word. The Bible is not a free-flowing narrative like a piece of poetry (although it contains poetry), it is also teaching, which has a main point that is supported most of the time by additional points – all in the context of what the Holy Spirit is sharing through the writer.

One of the great skills that God wants his children to develop is the ability to take that ten-ounce steak and divide it into bite-size pieces by learning to see those natural divisions in the Word of God. You can turn almost anywhere in the New Testament and see those natural divisions, but let me give one example. In Philippians 2:5-8, it says: "In your relationships with one another, have the same mindset as Christ Jesus: Who, being in very nature God, did not consider equality with God something to be used to his own advantage; rather, he made himself nothing by taking the very nature of a servant, being made in human likeness. And being found in appearance as a man, he humbled himself by becoming obedient to death — even death on a cross!" Read those four verses a couple of times and then try to find the natural divisions that highlight the main idea and the supporting ideas of that passage. Sometimes when we read this part of Philippians without looking at the context, we see verses 6-8 as a teaching about Jesus, and even though it is giving some amazing truths about Jesus, the context of the passage was about how the Philippians were treating each other! So, with this in mind, we see that the main idea is verse 2, "In your relationships with one another, have the same mindset as Christ Jesus." Once you've established the main idea, you then see that the following verses are supporting that idea, describing what exactly it means to have the mindset of Christ in our relationships with others.

Main Idea: (vs.5) "In your relationships with one another, have the same mindset as Christ"
Subpoint #1 (vs.6) "who did not consider equality with God something to be used to his own advantage"
Subpoint #2 (vs.7) "who made himself nothing by taking the very nature of a servant"
Subpoint #3 (vs.8) "he humbled himself by becoming obedient to death"

As you chew on those bite-size pieces, you begin to understand the deeper meaning of this passage:

| **Main Idea:** To be Christlike (have the same mindset as Christ) in my relationships with others I must: |
| **Subpoint #1:** Not rely on privilege |
| **Subpoint #2:** Intentionally take the nature of a servant |
| **Subpoint #3:** Have an obedience that is self-sacrificing. |

The Bible works on so many levels in the life of a Christian. While we should be constantly refreshing our spirit by reading through it, we must also pause on a daily basis and dive down into the real meaning of Scripture: rightly dividing the word of truth!

Principle #3: To Hear God's Voice In His Word We Must Be Willing To Obey His Word

There comes a point in every human relationship where a parent or a concerned friend realizes that it's useless to talk any further because there is obviously no intention on the part of the hearer to follow through and obey. Even though we understand this in the natural, we so often expect God to guide us even when our willingness to obey him is seen as an optional or circumstantial proposition.

The word "obedience" is not one you often hear in sermons or Christian books in our modern Christian culture. To Westerners, obedience seems to infringe on our personal rights; and in Eastern cultures, obedience has been used to manipulate and stifle individuality since childhood. The enemy has done an excellent job in causing the principle of obedience to seem like a negative principle, and he does this because he understands, much better than we, that obedience is more important than we realize. It's fascinating that in the New Testament, we are told that even Jesus, in his development as a human being, had to learn this principle. In the book of Hebrews it says, "Son though he was, he learned obedience from what he suffered" (Hebrews 5:80. That is quite an amazing statement, that even though Jesus was the third part of the Trinity and God from the beginning – as a person he had to learn obedience!

When the prophet Jeremiah stood, by the Lord's command, at the gates of the house of the Lord, he proclaimed these words to the people who were coming in to worship, "This is what the Lord Almighty, the God of Israel, says: Go ahead, add your burnt offerings to your other sacrifices and eat the meat yourselves! For when I brought your ancestors out of Egypt and spoke to them, I did not just give them commands about burnt offerings and sacrifices, but I gave them this command: Obey me, and I will be your God and you will be my people" (Jeremiah 7:22-23). Centuries before the coming of Jesus, the intention of God was clear: he didn't want to just give religious commands to be followed, he wanted to be obeyed! Not in the way that slaves obey their master, but an obedience that comes when he is our God and we are his people.

I have come to believe that obedience is the great forgotten key when it comes to Christian growth and discipleship in the 21st-century. Not an obedience that forces God to speak, or even an obedience that earns the right to hear him speak, but an obedience that shows God we are willing to follow through! It's no coincidence that when Jesus gave the parable about the man who built his house upon the sand and the man who built his house upon the rock, the one difference in the two structures was whether or not that word had been put into practice! Let's take a deeper look into why obedience is so important in our relationship with God, and why it determines whether he will continue to speak to us through his written word.

Obedience Is The True Measure Of Love

Love is a hard thing to measure. When we try to measure its depth through emotions or through promises, we can easily be deceived. Jesus, in the course of his ministry upon the Earth, had a lot of people who expressed their devotion and their desire to follow him. It's interesting that, for Jesus, there was only one true measure of their love – in the book of John he said, "If you love me, keep my commands" (John 14:15). In our modern Christian culture, it's all too easy to believe that the proof of our love for Jesus is only in how we feel towards him, but for Jesus, the bar is much higher than that! We must understand that hearing his voice is directly connected to loving him more and loving him more is directly connected to a determination to obey him.

The apostle John understood this and was pointing at this important principle when he said, "For this is the love of God, that we keep his commandments" (I John 5:3). In other words, this is what love really is, the essence and the true nature of love is to obey what he has commanded and to listen to every word from the mouth of God with a heart that says, "yes Lord." When the risen Jesus appeared before a somewhat discouraged Peter who had returned to his fishing business he asked three times, "Peter do you love me more than these?" The immediate response to Peter's declaration of love was, "Feed my sheep" (John 21:17). Again, our willingness to obey doesn't earn points with God but it does indicate better than anything else that we want to hear his voice simply because we love him.

Obedience Creates Authority

Who I'm willing to consistently listen to throughout my life is usually the one who has the most authority in my life. I listen carefully to the instructions of my boss, not because I particularly love the way he speaks but simply because he is an authority over me, he determines whether I will continue to keep my job. Growing up, I was willing to listen to my parents (at least some of the time) because they were the authority figures that I'd grown up with since childhood. Who we perceive as being in authority over us is usually who we are willing to carefully listen to. But what actually creates authority? When people discover that certain addictions or sinful practices seem to have absolute authority over their lives, what exactly has created that authority?

There is a passage in the book of Romans that gives an intriguing answer to that question, "Don't you know that when you offer yourselves to someone as obedient slaves, you are slaves of the one you obey – whether you are slaves to sin, which leads to death, or to obedience, which leads to righteousness?" (Romans 6:16). Tom Marshall, a gifted pastor and author from New Zealand always used to say that he could sum up those two verses in three words, "Obedience creates authority." The one you offer yourself to in obedience is the one who becomes your master. Whether it's slavery to sin or slavery to God – it is our obedience that creates the authority!

I had the privilege of seeing this principle worked out on a national scale in the 1980s when I lived in the Philippines during the last year of the 21-year reign of the dictator Ferdinand Marcos. It was quite eye-opening for an American to live in a dictatorship – the newspapers were filled with nothing but complimentary stories about President Marcos and his wife Imelda. There were special policemen at the airports who carefully examined each arriving visitor and the entire economy benefited and enriched the Marcos family. I was also there when the famous "People Power Revolution" took place in Manila and over one million Filipinos decided they would no longer obey his authority. As every street in Manila filled with people standing peacefully, saying, "We will no longer obey," the authority of a ruthless dictator just evaporated!

When we say that Jesus is Lord or that God is our authority, we sometimes are doing nothing more than just acknowledging his power in the universe, but for God to actually be the authority over our day-to-day lives, only our obedience can cause that to become a reality. Many Christians put the cart before the horse when they think to themselves, "If God demonstrates his authority then I will obey him." But the truth is that it's the other way around: I must demonstrate my obedience before God will manifest his authority in my life. The more that I obey his command to love him with all my heart, the greater authority his love has over my life. The more I obey his command to love my enemies, the greater authority he has over my enemies. The more I obey his command to be a servant to all, the more he is able, by his authority, to lift me up. Authority is only established through obedience!

Obedience Enables The Next Step

When reading God's Word and trying to discern what it is saying about the next step in your life, it's sometimes easy to overlook an important principle expressed in the book of Philippians where it says, "All of us, then, who are mature should take such a view of things. And if on some point you think differently, that too God will make clear to you. Only let us live up to what we have already attained" (Philippians 3:15-16). In other words, you've got to live out the last thing he said to you before he will say something new! It's very tempting to expect God to lay out our lives step-by-step without any real obedience required on our part, but it is actually obedience to the last step that enables the next!

In my life as a Jesus-follower on foreign fields, I've learned that before I could ever go into all the nations, I had to be obedient to the little steps that would lead to all the nations. For me, this meant being obedient to the idea of not laying up for myself treasures upon the Earth or being careful that I'm not serving two masters in my life. I discovered that when I was obedient in the little steps, it positioned me to be able to take the big step when God said, "Go." There are many well-meaning Christians who have a sincere heart to go into all the world and to be a witness for Jesus, but hearing that command is not enough, we must be willing to position ourselves through obedience to the little things if we are ever going to find the release to go.

If I truly want to attune my ear to hear God's voice on a daily basis, I must settle in my mind that the starting place is not found in mystical experiences or dreams or visions – the starting place is the written Word of God. This means I must be willing to read enough of his word that it's actually having an influence on my life: helping me to see the difference between soulish and spiritual ideas; shedding light on the true motivations of my heart. It means that I must also be willing to rightly divide the word of God, learning how to chew my meat and receive the nourishment that is needed from every word that proceeds from the mouth of God. It means that I must be determined to obey what I read, to learn obedience in the same way that Jesus learned obedience – with the understanding that obedience is the true measure of love and authority that also enables me to take the next step in following God's will.

A Plan for Bible Meditation

The term "meditation" is not something you hear too often in Christian circles. We have a tendency to think only of Eastern meditation or the New Age techniques that have become popular in our culture, but long before those things, God commanded us to meditate upon his word!

After the death of Moses, God began to instruct Joshua, the new leader, in all of the things he needed to become his successor. Along with his commands to be strong and courageous and to obey the law, God also said something which was crucial if Joshua was going to have the ability to be an effective leader. In the book of Joshua, God said these words, "Keep this book of the law always on your lips; meditate on it day and night, so that you may be careful to do everything written in it. Then you will be prosperous and successful" (Joshua 1:8). I find it interesting that the key to prosperity and success in the kingdom of God had very little to do with building organizations or finding ways to raise finances. In God's words to Joshua, prosperity and success were directly connected to his ability to meditate on God's word day and night! It's easy for us to assume that this word "meditate" just means to read or to study, but it's an unusual word in the Hebrew, *hagah,* which literally means, "to mutter or to murmur." What exactly was God asking Joshua to do, day and night, concerning his Word? When you think about it, the idea of murmuring or muttering something can be like repeating it over and over under your breath, and the amazing thing about the Word of God is that it will almost always open up and show you something much deeper than what was on the surface of the verse, if you are willing to give your full attention to one or two verses that you read in context, and begin to think deeply about what they are actually saying.

It's one of the strangest aspects of the Bible and, to me, one of the great proofs that it truly is a supernatural book. I've been teaching God's Word for over 30 years now, and when I look back on years of sermon preparation and lesson development, it amazes me that I can still – every day – look deeply into the word of God and see things there that speak something fresh to my heart. I believe that we give up too quickly when it comes to Bible reading and don't realize that there is a great difference between reading the Scripture and meditating on the Scripture – for it is there that we learn to hear

God's voice in God's Word! Let's unpack this command that God gave to Joshua and try to see a practical plan for Bible meditation.

Meditation Step #1:

After your daily Bible reading, choose one verse and write it at the beginning of your journal entry for that day. "Keep this book of the law always on your lips…"

I like the way that Eugene Peterson in his paraphrased Bible, *The Message*, renders this verse, "And don't for a minute let this book of the Revelation be out of mind." When God told Joshua to keep the law always on his lips, I don't believe that he meant Joshua was supposed to be constantly spouting Scripture to everyone he met, but that the Word of God was to never be far from his thoughts. That's a very noble sentiment, but in real life, I've discovered that the only way to *keep* God's Word in mind is to consistently *put* it into your mind for most of every day! So, assuming that you are someone who reads a bit of Scripture regularly, the first step in meditation is to choose a small part of it that you're going to hold in your mind. I'm not sure why but, for most of us, writing something down gives us a point of focus that we don't have if we just look at it on the printed page or try to hold it in our memory. Writing anchors our attention for a few moments, which enables us to then proceed to the next step in Bible meditation…

Meditation Step #2:

Ponder the verse, and ask the question: "What does this mean to me?" "Keep this book of the law always on your lips… meditate on it,"

This is an important question, because we so often have a tendency to only ask, "What does this mean?" instead of, "What does this mean to me?" This doesn't imply that we must find some elaborate interpretation that is out of context with the passage, but it does mean that we are allowing the Word of God to be living and active in our hearts. As an illustration, on the day that I was writing this part of the manuscript, I happened to be reading the ninth chapter of the Gospel of John. In the course of reading, I felt a nudge to go back and ponder verses 1-3, "As he went along, he saw a man blind from birth. His disciples asked him, 'Rabbi, who sinned, this man or his parents, that he was born blind?' 'Neither this man nor his parents sinned,' said Jesus, 'but this happened so that the works of God might be displayed in him'" (John 9:1-3). As I began to murmur (*hagah*) the last part of that verse, "...this happened so that the works of God might be displayed in him... this happened so that the works of God might be displayed in him... this happened so that the works of God might be displayed in him," it began to dawn on me that every weakness in our lives, though not caused by God, has a deep purpose in God's plan for our lives, to display clearly God's works! This led to the next step of my meditation...

Meditation Step #3:

Use the meaning of the verse to provide a structure for God to speak. "Keep this book of the law always on your lips; meditate on it... day and night,"

Notice in my illustration that there is a certain logic or structure found in the meaning of that verse:

— God didn't cause this infirmity

— God has a purpose for this infirmity

— God's works can be displayed through this infirmity

This provides a biblically-based structure through which God can speak directly to me. That morning, as I meditated on the passage in John 9, this is what I believe God spoke to my heart through the structure of the meaning of that verse:

"Every weakness in a human being, whether it's blindness or bad temper, has only one ultimate purpose in my kingdom: that the works of God might be displayed. Understand that the truth is: the greater the weakness, the greater the potential that my works can be displayed. Never be embarrassed by your shortcomings nor should you judge the shortcomings of others, for it is in a human being's weakness that my strength is made perfect." September 30, 2019

This understanding of God's ultimate purpose for human shortcomings and weaknesses was something that resonated in my mind throughout the day and it was a good word for someone who still feels unqualified even after thirty years of ministry.

Meditation Step #4:

Having now pondered the verse, look for ways to practice what you've meditated on. "Keep this book of the law always on your lips; meditate on it day and night, so that you may be careful to do everything written in it."

Notice that God didn't say to Joshua, "You might want to do everything written in it" – but that Joshua should "be careful to do everything written in it." As I mentioned earlier in the book, obedience today is one of the keys to hearing God tomorrow. We must never forget that God's word, when spoken to us, only has value if it's put into practice. In my illustration of what God happened to say to me on September 30, I found myself, throughout the day, seeing the Indian people that live in my neighborhood, not in terms of "Why are they suffering, Lord?" but instead, "Let your works be greatly manifest in their lives, Lord!"

Meditation step #1:

After your daily Bible reading, choose one verse and write it at the beginning of your journal entry for that day. "Keep this book of the law always on your lips…"

Meditation step #2:

Ponder the verse, and ask the question: "What does this mean to me?" "Keep this book of the law always on your lips… meditate on it,"

Meditation step #3:

Use the meaning of the verse to provide a structure for God to speak. "Keep this book of the law always on your lips; meditate on it… day and night,"

Meditation step #4:

Having now pondered the verse, look for ways to practice what you've meditated on. "Keep this book of the law always on your lips; meditate on it day and night, so that you may be careful to do everything written in it."

When King David said, "I will meditate on your precepts and fix my eyes on your ways" (Psalm 119:15 ESV), he made it clear that there is an undeniable link between meditating on God's word and being able to fix our eyes on God's ways. One of the great tragedies of our modern church culture is our attempt to determine God's ways while ignoring the important step of learning to meditate – hearing God's voice in God's Word.

Questions to Ponder

1. If you believe that "all Scripture is breathed out by God" how should that change the influence of Scripture in your daily life?

2. What is the difference between the two questions, "How much am I reading?" and "How well am I listening?"

3. How does the illustration of cutting up your food, chewing it, and digesting it, help you understand how to really digest the Word of God?

4. Why do you think that your willingness to obey is directly linked to your ability to hear God's Word?

5. What changes can you make to your daily Bible reading to include a time of meditating on God's Word?

Chapter Four

Prophesying to Yourself

The "Gifts of the Spirit" – a message of wisdom, message of knowledge; faith and healing, miracles and prophecy, distinguishing between spirits, speaking in different kinds of tongues and interpreting those tongues – has always been a controversial subject throughout the history of the church. There is controversy about whether it was only for the time of the apostles or for today, and even controversy about whether it was primarily for inside the church or out on the streets. But sometimes amidst all the controversy, we lose sight of the real purpose of these gifts which are firmly intertwined with the *work* of the Holy Spirit on Earth. When Jesus talked about this work of the Holy Spirit he said in the gospel of John, "But when he, the Spirit of truth, comes, he will guide you into all the truth. He will not speak on his own; he will speak only what he hears, and he will tell you what is yet to come. He will glorify me because it is from me that he will receive what he will make known to you. All that belongs to the Father is mine. That is why I said the Spirit will receive from me what he will make known to you" (John 16:13-15).

Notice that this important work of guiding into all truth was done through the medium of words! Jesus pointed out that the work of the Holy Spirit was to speak only what he hears and to tell them what is yet to come. The Holy Spirit would glorify Jesus not just through raw power but by speaking to them the things that God wanted them to know. Even in the list of the gifts of the Holy Spirit in I Corinthians 12, many of the ones listed have to do with God *speaking* through words of wisdom and knowledge and different kinds of tongues and the interpretation of those tongues and prophecy.

One of the things that I've learned in the last several years of mentoring others is that self-discipline alone will not bring us to a place of consistently taking dictation each morning – it requires the gifts of the Holy Spirit! In the past ten years of mentoring, I've seen some people grow rapidly in their ability to hear God, while others struggle just to have a quiet time on a consistent basis. It was tempting to just write it off to different types of personality, but I've become convinced that hearing God has nothing to do with the way that a person is wired, it has everything to do with our ability to embrace the working of the gifts of the Holy Spirit within ourselves! One of the reasons why so many struggle with the gifts of the Holy Spirit is that we see them only in the context of ministry to others. In charismatic churches, that usually means laying hands on someone and praying that the Holy Spirit will work to bring a miracle or healing or the word of wisdom or prophecy to that person. It's easy to delegate that kind of ministry only to leaders in the church and miss the fact that the gifts of the Spirit actually work in two directions: outward to others but also inward to ourselves!

I've always found it intriguing that, after describing the gifts of the Holy Spirit to the Corinthian Christians, Paul told them to, "Pursue love and earnestly desire the spiritual gifts, especially that you may prophesy" (I Corinthians 14:1). You might think that Paul would have placed a greater emphasis on gifts like healing or faith or miracles, but for some reason, he underlined the importance of prophecy. The word he was using here in the Greek is an interesting one, the word *propheteuo*, which *Vine's Expository Dictionary* defines primarily as "telling forth the divine counsels." While it is true that God's divine counsel might include the foretelling of future events, God's counsel is much more than that! And it is here that we begin to see the separation in our understanding of how we get counsel from God. Most Christians see God's counsel as coming from sources such as their pastor or friends, or even through feelings and circumstances, but we often don't connect the fact that God's divine counsel (showing us what to do and how to respond) is a prophetic gift of the Holy Spirit!

About two years into our eleven-year journey in Russia, my wife and I began to have a heavy burden concerning the huge percentage of abortions that were taking place in the nation at that time. In communist days, it was just about the only form of birth control available, and even after the fall of the Soviet Union, an average Russian woman would have several abortions in her lifetime. We started to think about setting up a pregnancy counseling ministry connected to the church we were planting, but as we listened to God in our journaling times, we were surprised to find that his answer was a resounding "wait." We weren't really sure what we were waiting for, but we had a feeling that God wanted to use us in a different way than the traditional Christian approach to pregnancy counseling. He continued to say "wait" to us for the rest of that year, and the following year we struggled through two early-term miscarriages. The second one put Vicki in the hospital (a cultural experience to say the least). As she was the first-ever American to be a patient in that hospital, the director took personal care of her and did such a wonderful job that we became friends.

Some time after that, we felt that God was showing us there was a point of contact between the Christian church and the Russian government in our vision for the nation – stopping abortion! The Russian Federation had for several decades been experiencing a negative growth rate and statistics were indicating that in the next fifty years there would not be enough Russian citizens to maintain such things as a strong military or a stable infrastructure. We felt from the Lord that we were to contact the chief doctor over the public hospitals in that region of Perm, and to our surprise, he turned out to be our friend, the local doctor who had treated Vicki – God had promoted him at just the right time! We presented to him the idea of a partnership between our non-profit (which was already visiting hospitals) and the city government to set up pregnancy counseling offices in the main hospitals where most abortions took place. He countered with a proposal that turned out to be much more effective, to set up our offices in the government-run women's consultation clinics where women got pregnancy tests and considered their options. After several years, we had four different pregnancy counseling offices operating with Christian volunteers who were able to offer an abortion option, as well as support for any who desired it.

That story is important, not because it showcases our organizational skills (we would have tried to do that ministry in the traditional way if we had not been taking dictation), but because I believe it illustrates the working of the gifts of the Holy Spirit. The Spiritual gift of the "word of knowledge" is usually defined as being shown something by the Holy Spirit that you had no knowledge of in the natural. We hear the exciting stories of people having their "mail read" by prophetic preachers in conferences, but shouldn't we consider the fact that the real purpose of the gift of the word of knowledge is not to impress you with what God knows about you, but to lead you into things you cannot yet see? When we were considering crisis pregnancy centers we had not yet encountered Vicki's doctor and we had no personal knowledge of the government's concern about the nation's negative growth rate, but as those two lines began to converge, the gift of the Holy Spirit prepared us to do something that we had no future knowledge of.

The spiritual gift of a "word of wisdom" is usually defined as being given wisdom from the Holy Spirit on how to respond in certain situations, and although we have a tendency to usually substitute advice for waiting on the Holy Spirit, should we consider the fact that this gift works best when we are taking dictation? As a pastor, I routinely discovered that I didn't really have a lot of wisdom to offer when it came to the difficult situations that people face in their lives, but as I began to allow the Holy Spirit to speak to me about them in my journal, I found a wisdom in pastoring them that I could never have attained in the natural. Sometimes, it was insight into what their real needs were, but other times I heard wisdom that was completely counterintuitive to my usual advice. I discovered that when I need God's wisdom, either as a pastor, a parent, or a husband, God does not answer by pouring some substance labeled "wisdom" into my brain, but by speaking wise words that can shape how I might effectively minister to another.

The Apostle Paul instructed his flock in the book of I Corinthians to, "Pursue love and earnestly desire the spiritual gifts, especially that you may prophesy" (I Corinthians 14:1), but those words must be seen in the context of what prophecy really means: *Propheteuo*, God's divine counsel. I believe that God wants to completely reframe what it means to emphasize the gifts of the Holy Spirit in the church, as well as what it means to be a "spirit-filled" Christian. As someone who was saved into the Pentecostal tradition, I cherish many of the experiences I had in those days. But the time has come for us to realize that God is not calling us just to have an experience in the Holy Spirit; he is, instead, calling us to have a deeper experience with God himself through the speaking of the Holy Spirit! To prophesy to yourself does not mean that you work up your emotions or even that you try to predict your own future, it means something much more important than that – for when you prophesy to yourself you are actually ministering to yourself!

While it is true that the Bible instructs us to be more concerned with others than we are with ourselves, that doesn't mean that we neglect caring for our inner man any more than we would neglect caring for the needs of our outer man. When you read Paul's description of the purpose of prophecy in I Corinthians it's easy to read into that verse something that's actually not there in the original language. In the New International Version, it says, "But the one who prophesies speaks to people for their strengthening, encouraging and comfort" (I Corinthians 14:3). The phrasing gives you the idea that prophecy is primarily speaking to other people. While it is certainly true that prophecy is often directed to others, the original word in the Greek is the word *anthrōpos*, which is the word "human being." The gift of prophecy is God's way of speaking to the human race, whether it is to others or to oneself! And if we take this description and apply it not just towards ministry to others, but also as ministry to ourselves, it gives us three ways of understanding how prophesying to yourself works:

#1: The Ministry of Building Up

(I Corinthians 14:3) "But the one who prophesies speaks to people for their... strengthening"

The Greek word that is being translated "strengthening" in the NIV is *oikodomē*, which is the common Greek word for "building something." Sometimes we get the idea that the main work of the Holy Spirit is to just give us the strength that we need in our lives, but the truth about the work of the Holy Spirit is that God wants to do more than just give us strength, he wants to build us up. There have been times in my life where, if God had strengthened and fortified me in ministry, it would have been a disaster! Strength would have enabled me to hold on to things that really needed to change in my ministry.

There is a tendency in modern Christian culture to see our salvation as the endgame instead of the beginning of a lifetime of building. When Paul said in Philippians 2:12 that they were to work out their own salvation "with fear and trembling" he didn't mean that they were to try to earn their salvation each day, but to allow their salvation to be the starting place that God would build on every day of their lives. When I'm learning, through the gift of prophecy, to allow God's divine counsel into my mind on a regular basis it will always cause there to be the building up and expanding of my Christian character. We often only think of "building up" in the context of enlarging our ministry, but the truth is that all ministry is utterly dependent on learning to let God build up our foundation. By foundation, I mean our basic understanding of who God is and what he thinks of us; our ability to hear his voice and to pray with authority and maturity. Without that broad foundation of character, ever-increasing ministry or career or responsibility will always reach a point where it will topple over! I've always believed that the main purpose of my journal that I've kept for thirty years is not knowing the future or even receiving directions but hearing God's divine counsel concerning how much he loves me and how valuable I am in his eyes. Only this has been able to build my foundation to the point where I could live in the slums of the Philippines in my 30s, or move to a city in Russia in my 40s or to settle into India in my mid-60s. Thirty years of prophesying to myself has, without a doubt, built a foundation that God could build upon!

The next two words in Paul's description of how prophecy ministers to others and to ourselves are the Greek words *paraklesis* and *paramythia*. Notice that they both start with the word *para* which means "beside or near" but each describes a different function of the gift of prophecy.

#2: The Ministry of Drawing Near

(I Corinthians 14:1) "But the one who prophesies speaks to people for their strengthening... encouraging."

71

The word being translated "encouraging" is the Greek word, *paraklesis* which literally means *para* (beside or near) and *kleo* (to call), in other words, to *call* near. Although I am no Bible translator, I find that while it is indeed encouraging when God draws near, the literal meaning of *paraklesis* has a more far-reaching meaning: the act of prophecy (whether to others or to oneself) has the effect of drawing us nearer to God! It's important to understand that I'm not saying that God dwells far away and has to be summoned by the gift of prophecy, but that the very act of listening to his voice *summons us* closer to him!

Along with the many blessings that have come with the charismatic movement, one of the unfortunate misunderstandings is that the way we draw closer to God is primarily through our emotions. Sensing God can often arouse emotions, so it's perfectly human to think that if I can arouse my emotions through worship or prayer then I will be able to sense his presence again in a more intimate way. Many have discovered, however, that maintaining high emotions in our Christian walk is unrealistic and leads to either disillusionment or duplicity in the way we present ourselves to others. That is precisely why drawing near to God is so dependent on the gifts of the Holy Spirit. Even Jesus himself called the Holy Spirit the *Parakletos* – the one who comes beside us to help us in our knowledge of God!

I've noticed in my Christian walk that I sometimes get turned around in my understanding of my relationship with God. It's easy to think that I must draw near to him before I will be able to hear him better, but I've discovered that just the opposite is true: only when I sit down in my quiet time, determined to hear him better do I find the Holy Spirit performing the ministry of *paraklesis,* drawing me closer to the Father! One of the most common struggles that people have, when they begin to try to take dictation, is that they believe they have to "feel something" from God before they can begin to hear the voice of God in his Word. All I feel is sleepy when I sit down most mornings for my quiet time, but as I begin to allow the gift of prophecy to flow from my pen to myself, I find that I'm always drawn closer to the Father.

#3: *The Ministry of the Still Small Voice*

(I Corinthians 14:3) "But the one who prophesies speaks to people for their strengthening, encouraging... and comfort."

This is that second *para* (beside or near) word, only this time it is connected with the Greek word *muthos* which means "to speak." In other words, this word that is translated in most Bibles as "comfort" is one that means "to *speak* near." Again, while it is very comforting when God speaks in our ear, *paramythia* has a much more far-reaching meaning.

Anyone who has ever tried to attune their ear to the voice of God knows exactly what the Bible means when it says that God speaks with a still small voice. There have been times when I've wondered why God chooses to speak in this way, it's not that he's weak or has laryngitis, but in his wisdom, he chooses a small voice over a big voice. And because this is true, it means that we need the gifts of the Holy Spirit to amplify that voice in our spiritual hearing. In mentoring people, I've often had people say to me, "I waited before God but he didn't say anything to me this week." In response I will sometimes point out that just waiting is not enough, we need to remember to say, "Come Holy Spirit and operate in me your speaking gifts." We certainly do that when we're prophesying over other people. We would never try to do ministry in our own strength and we are quick to call out to God, but when it comes to ministering to ourselves, we sometimes forget that we are just as dependent on the Spirit's gifts.

I believe that this word, translated "comfort" *(paramythia)*, also has a deeper meaning than just the voice of God whispering into our ear. It also points to a certain level of intimacy where God is speaking only to me with words that apply only to me and no one else. So much of our ability to obey God rests on this kind of intimacy, for I will never be able to have faith in someone that I don't know well. If you think about it, there are really two kinds of relationships that Christians have with God: a Lord-relationship and a Father-relationship. Anyone who has committed their lives to Jesus starts off with a Lord-relationship: he is now the Lord of our lives and we are willing to do whatever he commands us to do. But many Christians don't realize that there is a deeper kind of relationship that God wants to have with us, one so intimate that it's very similar to the relationship that a father has with his children. One of the great keys to Christian growth is to allow God to begin to transition us from a Lord-relationship to a Father-relationship in the way that we understand him. Being able to hear those intimate words of a father is a big part of making that transition.

When Paul said, "Pursue love and earnestly desire the spiritual gifts, especially that you may prophesy" (I Corinthians 14:1), he wasn't really speaking to professional evangelists or conference speakers (they didn't exist yet). He was speaking to young Christians who would only grow if they pursued the two primary things that lead to Christian growth: love and the gifts of the Holy Spirit. There are certainly times when we need God's prophet to stand and to declare God's word to a nation, but I believe that the much more pressing need is that we learn, through the gift of prophecy, to daily hear the divine counsel of God.

Questions to Ponder

1. How does the meaning of the word prophecy (telling forth the divine counsels) change your understanding of what it means to prophesy to others as well as to yourself?

2. How can the gifts of the Holy Spirit, and not just feelings, help you in developing a more consistent quiet time and journaling time?

3. When prophesying to yourself, why is building up more important than being strengthened?

4. What is the difference between trying to draw near to God in quiet time as opposed to allowing the Holy Spirit to draw near?

5. What is the difference between waiting for God to speak in your quiet time and asking God to speak through the gifts of the Holy Spirit?

Chapter Five

Making Decisions Based on What God Is Saying

The ability to make a decision is something that is very uniquely human. Animals can make basic "hardwired" decisions, such as fight or flight, but when it comes to choosing which direction to take on the path of life, it seems that human beings alone have the free will to choose.

If you think about it, our free will to choose is very much a double-edged sword. Authentic love, whether it's loving God or our neighbor as ourselves, must be the product of choice if it's going to be genuine. Love that is forced out of someone is, by definition, not love at all. But, at the same time, on the other edge of that double-edged sword, we discover that a free will to choose means that I can choose to disobey God, and because he has given me that free will, he will honor that choice even if it breaks his heart. Our free will to choose also has the subtle ability to alter the direction of our lives. Even little choices, such as the decision to be kind to those who have less than I have, or my decision to communicate with my wife, alter basic things in my character and personality. It's even more obvious in big decisions, such as who I should marry or what career I should pursue, or even what ministry God has called me to. Exercising my free will to choose can set me on a path that can define the direction and character of my entire life.

People have many different methods that they use in order to make a decision. Some people decide according to what "feels best" in their hearts, while others are logical decision-makers, weighing up the pros and cons in order to determine the right path. Some people prefer to have others make their decisions for them, while still others are so driven by circumstances in their lives that they don't feel they've ever really had a choice at all. Christians understand (in theory) that every major decision in life should be prayed over, but when you look closely into the expression "I prayed over it," you find that quite often people just mean that they presented the decision to God and now the ball is in his court! Most of us have discovered that when we are faced with a major decision, it is very difficult, at that point, to pray and receive direction from God. Our minds are consumed with all of the possibilities and we feel pressured to give an answer, so we usually end up falling back on doing nothing more than hoping that God will stop us if we're wrong!

If we choose to really believe what God said through the prophet Jeremiah, "For I know the plans I have for you, declares the Lord, plans for welfare and not for evil, to give you a future and a hope" (Jeremiah 29:11 ESV), then doesn't it make sense to find out what those plans are before making life-altering decisions? Most Christians would answer "yes" to that question, but the problem is in how we interpret God's plan. On one side of the spectrum are those who believe that God has a general plan for our lives, but it's up to us to fill in the details. One might say, "God wants me to be good, so as long as I do something with all my heart and don't hurt others then I'm following his plan for my life." On the other side of the spectrum are those who live in terror of taking even one step off the path that God has created for them; they can become paralyzed by fear and even obsessive to the point of needing to hear God's voice on what to eat for breakfast that morning. But if we move to the "radical middle" of that spectrum we discover that God wants to slowly begin to show us, on a daily basis, his plan for our lives and gradually bring it into focus long before a decision has to be made.

My wife and I have experienced this truth many times over the past 26 years. Just recently we experienced again the crucial importance of making a decision based on what God is saying. In 2014, while still pastoring the Atlanta Vineyard, we started to hear in our journals the beginnings of God's call to India. Over the course of that year, we recorded so many journal entries that we decided to take a family vacation to Bangalore, India to visit some friends and take a look at this place God was speaking about. Over the next five years, we led two teams from our church back to Bangalore as God continued to speak hundreds of times in our prayer journals that India would be our next assignment – but we had to wait until he said, "Go." Those five years were probably the longest that I've ever waited for God's next step, and honestly, there were times when I wondered if the door would ever open.

During those years, God instructed us concerning several things that seemed unrelated to India. First, Vicki heard in her journal the Lord challenging her to go back to school and get her master's degree in education. Meanwhile, I had numerous journal entries about the church that I pastored, that the next pastor must be an African American pastor and the Atlanta Vineyard must be at the forefront of growth in ethnic diversity. About three years into this process we ordained an African American leader in our church to be the volunteer associate pastor, and the year after that Vicki graduated from the University of Georgia with her master's degree. It's important to point out that none of these things were being done according to some master plan that we had to transition back to the foreign field; they were decisions that were made almost exclusively according to what we were hearing in our prayer journals. Even though the door still seemed more closed than ever for India and there didn't seem to be any way to live there long-term, we continued to have entry after entry assuring us that we were to wait for God to make a way.

In January 2019 I heard several times in my journal that things were going to start happening quickly – and in March of that year, things did indeed start to happen! Vicki attended a large international TESOL conference in Atlanta and visited a booth that was being run by the U.S. State Department promoting its English Language Fellow Program. We were surprised to discover that the United States sends (and pays for) a small number of teachers annually to go into universities around the world to teach English. We heard God's release to have Vicki apply for this program (even though it was rather late) and to specify that we were only interested in India. We didn't have high expectations that anything would happen, but to our surprise, she was offered a post in India in May. We were given only three days to make a decision that would have us leaving for India in three months! I'm pretty sure that if I had not had five years of journal entries confirming that I was to resign the church and move to India I would not have been able to take that step, but we knew that God had spoken, so it was much easier to make the decision. As I look back on our latest experience of making a decision based on what God is saying, I can see a kind of pattern that I think points out some general principles that are also reflected in the words of the wisest king who ever lived, "Trust in the Lord with all your heart, and do not lean on your own understanding. In all your ways acknowledge him, and he will make straight your paths" (Proverbs 3:5-6). Let's unpack these words and try to understand some principles on how to make a decision based on what God is saying.

Decision-Making Principle #1: My Level of Trust Must Increase

"Trust in the Lord with all your heart..." (Proverbs 3:5)

If you think about it, before you can commit yourself to making decisions based on what God is saying, you have to take a hard look at where you place your trust. With many Christians, this is the "elephant in the room" in their relationship with God. Many believers have the unspoken fear that if they fully trust God with the direction of their lives, he will lead them to do something that they don't really want to do. It's easy to deceive oneself into believing that this attitude is just healthy caution when at its core, it is really rebellion! For others, trusting God can only be approached if there are plenty of safety nets in the form of alternate plans and strategies.

In the five years that we waited for God to open the door for India, I realize now that it was not just five years of waiting, but five years of God bringing us to a place where we could trust him with all of our heart. Vicki learned to trust him as she returned to college in her early 60s and I learned to trust him as I prepared to work myself out of a job in a society where there aren't a lot of jobs for those who have reached retirement age. Looking back, I realize that it probably required five years of work before we could truly trust God with all our heart in his call to India. It's not a coincidence that in Proverbs it doesn't say "trust in the Lord as much as you can "but "trust in the Lord with all of your heart," which means a total commitment to trusting him. When you do anything with all of your heart it means that there is no part of your heart left over for anything else.

So how do I increase my level of trust in God?

Trust Increases When Intimacy Increases

Trust is not something that you can increase with your willpower. I might point to a perfect stranger and say, "You can trust that man with all of your heart." Even though you might start a relationship with that person based on my recommendation, you will only be able to trust him yourself after you have grown in your relationship with him. One of the beautiful things to be found in meditating upon God's word is that it helps to build a much clearer picture of God's character. As I learn to spend time with God every morning and let him speak the words of a father over my life, the quality of my relationship with him grows, and as a result, my ability to trust him grows as well. If we approach taking dictation only in the context of being shown what to do, we will never be able to get our trust to the point of making decisions based on what he has said. Trust only increases when intimacy increases.

Trust Increases When Visibility Increases

It's no secret that many people have a very distorted picture of God in their heart of hearts. To some, he is an uncompromising judge that will punish every transgression, to others he is a cruel and fickle deity that causes things to happen that are hard to explain. Many have such an unhealthy fear of God that their main goal is to simply stay out of his way! Sometimes we only think of Jesus in the context of Savior, but there was another deeper reason why God chose to become flesh and dwell among us. Jesus said it this way in John 12:45, "The one who looks at me is seeing the one who sent me." That statement is either the craziest thing any human being has ever said, or it is the greatest key to developing a clear picture of what God is really like. Over the years as a pastor, I've had many people say to me, "How can I trust God when he is invisible and indiscernible in my daily life?"

The answer I give them is that he is far from invisible; we have a living picture of every aspect of his character in Jesus the Son! When one of his disciples, Philip, asked Jesus to show them the Father, he responded by saying a very strange thing, "Don't you know me, Philip, even after I have been among you such a long time? Anyone who has seen me has seen the Father. How can you say, 'Show us the Father'? Don't you believe that I am in the Father, and that the Father is in me?" (John 14:9-10). In other words: "I can't believe that you're asking me to show you the Father when the Father, every aspect of him, is on display in me!" Anyone who desires to have a clear and detailed picture of God needs to look no further than the Gospels. So often we read about Jesus only to learn his teachings or to be comforted by his words, without realizing that the most important reason for focusing on Jesus in the Gospels is to see God more clearly – for the more visible that he becomes the more my trust will increase!

Trust Increases When Unbelief Decreases

I've come to believe that at the root of much of the fear and the insecurity that is in my life is not some basic flaw in my character, but a deep and hidden core of unbelief. When God shows us that core of unbelief we usually have two choices: we either take ownership of it and repent before him in humility or we quickly cover it up again with excuses that say, "Well, I'm only human."

There is a lesson to be learned in the story of the father who brought his afflicted child, who was in convulsions, rolling on the ground and foaming at the mouth, before Jesus. He said to Jesus, "If you can do anything, take pity on us and help us." Jesus answered, "If you can? Everything is possible for one who believes" (Mark 9: 22-23). Notice the declaration that the boy's father makes, which seems to be the key to his son's healing, "Immediately the boy's father exclaimed, I do believe, help me overcome my unbelief" (Mark 9:24). In other words, he was saying, "I will believe to the level that I'm able, but I choose to trust you to help me move to a deeper level of belief!" So often when we reach the limit of our ability to believe the Lord, the boundary line that separates belief from unbelief, we have a tendency to stop there, not realizing that it is possible to step over that line if we are willing to cry out to the Lord, "Help me in my unbelief!" It requires little trust to walk in the things that I already believe are possible, but if I'm willing to risk taking even one step into the realm that I don't believe is possible, I will discover much about what it means to trust in the Lord.

Decision-Making Principle #2: Look at What I'm Leaning On

"Trust in the Lord with all your heart… and do not lean on your own understanding." (Proverbs 3:5)

Notice that Solomon did not say, "Do not have your own understanding" but, "Do not *lean* on your own understanding." In the Hebrew, the word that's being translated "lean" is the word *shaan* which is defined as meaning "to support oneself." It's human nature to develop throughout our life a "support system" which gives us a sense of safety, and the way that we make decisions is very much dependent on what that support system is. It's easy to let our understanding be the structure that keeps us stable… until something happens that is outside of our understanding! The hard truth is that we have a lot of evidence in the Bible of God speaking to people and instructing them to do things that were far beyond their level of understanding. Abraham and Sarah heard God say they would have a child in their old age, and as they waited many years for that promise to be fulfilled, they had to learn to not rely on their support system of understanding. Moses heard God say that he would deliver his people from slavery, but the way that God brought about that deliverance would never have fit into the structure of his understanding of kingdoms and politics as a former prince of Egypt.

So how do we become people who have understanding but do not lean on it?

Let Humility Temper Your Understanding

The more that the human race advances in science and technology, the more we discover how little we really know or understand about the universe around us. Towards the end of the 19th century, a group of scientists publicly declared that most of what can be discovered in the world around us has already been revealed. Little did they know that in the next hundred years breakthroughs would be made that would change almost every area of scientific understanding. In an article I read not long ago in *Scientific American*, Caleb Scharf[2] gave a list of all the things we don't know about the world around us: we don't know what "dark matter" is, even though it constitutes 27.6% of what the universe is made of. We don't know whether life exists anywhere else in the universe even though we've been looking and listening for many decades now. We don't understand how the quantum world works, a place where things can seem to be in two places at once. We don't understand our own human biology, where ten trillion human cells are augmented, exploited, and nurtured by a hundred trillion microbial cells. We don't understand how our own Earth works, how rolls of convecting, conducting material in the outer core that generate our planetary magnetic field. And in his conclusion, he makes what I think is an important statement: "But the point is not to get despondent, because this ignorance is a *beautiful* thing. It's what ultimately drives science and it's what makes the universe truly awe-inspiring."

I would also add that ignorance is a beautiful thing because it not only drives our desire to learn more about God's creation, it also creates a real *humility* that can keep us from constructing too large

---

2   Scharf, C. (2014). "This is what we don't know about the Universe." *Scientific American*. Retrieved in January 2020 from: https://blogs. scientificamerican.com/life-unbounded/this-is-what-we-done28099t-know-about-the-universe/

of a support system of our own understanding. King David pointed out in the book of Psalms that, "He leads the humble in what is right and teaches the humble his way" (Psalm 25:9 ESV). In our modern church culture, it's easy to miss the connection between these two concepts: God's guidance, showing us the right decision to make, and the humility that must be in our heart, if we are going to learn how **not** to lean on our own understanding. There is perhaps also a second answer to the question: How do we become people who have understanding but do not lean on it?

Do Not Be Conformed To The World

Sometimes when we read Scripture verses like Romans 12:2 where it says, "do not be conformed to this world, but be transformed by the renewal of your mind," it's easy to interpret that as meaning, "Do not be conformed to the sin of this world." A better understanding would be to realize it means "do not be conformed to the *ways* of this world." When it comes to decision-making, we grow up exposed every day to the way the world makes decisions. In the world, decisions are made according to what feels best, or what is in your best interest, or what is the most logical pathway. It's easy to find oneself leaning on the way the world understands things without even realizing that you're doing it. That is why the ongoing daily transformation that takes place when we give God time every day is so important. Most people don't have the inner strength to force their minds not to conform with the ways of the world, but the Holy Spirit has the transforming power to change our understanding of the way of doing things! And if you take a second look at this Scripture in the book of Romans, you see that it is directly connected to making decisions based on what God is saying. Let's look at it again in context: (Romans 12:2) "Do not conform to the pattern of this world but be transformed by the renewing of your mind. Then you will be able to test and approve what God's will is—his good, pleasing, and perfect will." Notice in this verse that only *then*, when your mind is transformed into a place where it's not conforming to the ways of the world, can you really test and approve God's will in any decision.

Decision-Making Principle #3: Acknowledge God in all Your Ways

"Trust in the Lord with all your heart, and do not lean on your own understanding; in all your ways acknowledge him, and he will make straight your paths" (Proverbs 3:5-6).

It's easy to say, "I will not lean on my own understanding," but the real test is to see if we are willing to "acknowledge him" by waiting for him to speak! In the Hebrew, that word "acknowledge" is the word, *yada* which is a verb that means "to know; to ascertain by seeing." So often we think of acknowledging the Lord only in terms of conceding that he is Lord, but Solomon understood that in order for God to make our paths straight, we have to know, in a very concrete way, how to acknowledge him.

What does it mean to acknowledge him in all your ways?

Acknowledge Him By Creating A Prayer Buffer

I believe that a prayer buffer (a period of time for seeking God's will) inserted between an idea and a decision is one of the most concrete ways that a believer can truly acknowledge that Jesus is Lord. How many decisions might have been very different in our lives if we had been willing to acknowledge that our understanding can't be leaned on and that we needed a period of time to know and to perceive what God was saying?

In our case, it was quite a large prayer buffer of five years between the idea of going to India and actually getting on the plane, but looking back, I can see that God in his wisdom knew it was going to take time to bring various things into place in our lives before we would be able to live long-term in India. As former missionaries, it would've been easy to have come up with our own plan: going in and out of the country on tourist visas or trying to get a business visa, but God said, "Wait" because time was needed in order for us to go in the way that he had planned. As a pastor, I've been in many leadership meetings where we brainstormed together and filled up a whiteboard with ideas on where the church should go and so I was often frustrated over the fact that those ideas never seemed to get off the whiteboard! In 2012, when I became the pastor of the Atlanta Vineyard, I made the decision to open every leadership meeting with one question: "What is God saying about our church?" I believe that this helped us to focus more on what God was saying and less on good ideas; so our policy was to always take every proposal and lay it before the Lord for one month before making a decision. If we didn't hear anything specific from God, then the good idea would remain only a good idea.

When faced with a major decision, I often counsel people to acknowledge God in a concrete way by creating space between the idea and the actual moment of making a decision. Not a space of passively waiting but, what a friend of mine used to call "actively listening." This is the practice of actively writing down each morning what you feel the Lord might be saying to your heart, but also laying on the altar your own ideas of what should be done. It's an attitude that says, "I'm not going to make this decision unless I hear from you, God."

Acknowledge That He Is The Lord of The Road

The phrase translated "all your ways" in the Hebrew is the word *derek* which literally means "a road." Figuratively it's used in the Bible to describe a course of life or a mode of action. Acknowledging the Lord in all your ways is much more than just recognizing that he is with you on your way, but that *the way itself* belongs to him! The road we are walking on is his property as the Lord of the Road and he has every right to determine the direction that road takes in our life! When we say, "My life is yours Lord, we mean more than just our physical selves, but also the path of life that we are pursuing. Solomon, the wisest king who ever lived, understood this when he said in Proverbs 16:9 (NLT), "We can make our plans, but the Lord determines our steps." In other words, I can plan how things might work out in my life, but it is the Lord who has the right to determine the direction of my steps!

When I became a Christian in 1976, I assumed that the direction my life would take would be in Christian music. I had been a semi-professional harmonica player before coming to Christ, and within a few months, I was in a Christian rock 'n' roll band playing in public parks and preaching the Gospel. The band was starting to become more popular and I was certainly enjoying myself, but in my young Christian heart, there was a deep desire to truly acknowledge God in all my ways (even in my harmonica). One day God said to me, "My way for you is not the way of music." I had just started learning how to have consistent quiet times and I was certainly a novice at taking dictation, but again and again, God challenged me to acknowledge him in all my ways by putting the harmonica on the altar. For me it was a very difficult struggle because playing the harmonica was about the only thing I was good at; yet, patiently and persistently, God asked me to acknowledge his Lordship by taking another path.

I finally submitted and told the guys in the band that I would be leaving – and didn't play one note on the harmonica for the next 10 years. During that time, I discovered to my amazement that God's road was one of learning how to teach his Word and, eventually, to go into all the world with his Word. I honestly believe that if I had not been willing to acknowledge God in all my ways, I would have taken much longer to discover the road that I've been walking on for the past 43 years.

Acknowledge Him By Learning to See What He Is Doing Around You

If you think about it, decision-making is more than just deciding on a master plan and moving towards it, life is lived from day to day and there are many small decisions we make every moment that can't be anticipated in a prayer journal. That's why it's so important to realize that God is not just present with you in your quiet time, he is all around you in every moment of your day. We know it's true because Jesus gave us an interesting glimpse into how this worked out in his own life. In John 5:19 he said, "Very truly I tell you, the Son can do nothing by himself; he can do only what he sees his Father doing, because whatever the Father does the Son also does." This statement presents a much different view of Jesus than the one that people might imagine about him. All that he did each day, every decision that he made and every action that he took was not on his own initiative, he could only do what he saw the Father doing. That is taking the practice of acknowledging God in all your ways to its highest level! So often when we read those words, it's tempting to think, "Well, that was Jesus, no one else can only do what he sees the Father doing," but the truth is there was nothing in the life of Jesus that was unique only to Jesus, he even said once that, "Whoever believes in me will do the works I have been doing, and they will do even greater things than these, because I am going to the Father" (John 14:12). So, if we acknowledge God by deciding we're only going to do what we see the Father doing, the question presents itself – "how can we see what the Father is doing?" As Henry Blackaby said in his groundbreaking book *Experiencing God,*

"You see what God is doing when you look for things that only God can do."[3]

When Jesus was describing to his disciples the kind of work that the Holy Spirit would do upon the Earth, it's interesting to note that the Holy Spirit's work was not just in believers but also in all of the people of the world. He said in John 16:8 "When he comes, he will prove the world to be in the wrong about sin and righteousness and judgment." That statement points to at least three things that only God can do through his Holy Spirit in the world around us:

1. When you observe someone who's beginning to realize that he is in the wrong in his understanding of sin (that sin is not just bad behavior but missing the mark) you are seeing something that only God can do. The way that we acknowledge God in that moment of recognition is to do what Jesus did: to join ourselves to what we see God doing, taking a few minutes of our time to share not only the definition of sin but the solution to sin in and through Jesus Christ.

2. When you realize in a conversation with another person that he is starting to recognize the fact that his own righteousness will never be enough to bring him closer to God, you are seeing the clear evidence of something that only God can do. To acknowledge God is to not just recognize what is happening but to ask God, "Do you want to use me in this work that you're doing in this person?"

3. When you see that a friend or family member is starting to realize that they are accountable for their life's decisions and

---

[3] Blackaby, H.T. (2008). *Experiencing God: Knowing and Doing the Will of God.* USA: B & H Publishing.

actions and there begins to be a stirring in their conscience, you are seeing the Father at work. To acknowledge God is to show someone how Jesus took our place.

Even though this book is about taking dictation, hearing God in our quiet times and making a record of what we're hearing, to acknowledge him in *all* our ways means that we must go beyond the inner room of our prayer times and hear also what God is saying in his *actions* in the lives of men.

I believe that God is calling his church in the 21st century to honestly examine the fact that to say we are followers of Jesus, without learning how to make decisions based on what he is saying, is not really following him at all! I also believe that God is wanting to bring Christians into a place of much greater confidence in their Christian walk, a confidence not found in leaning on our own understanding but a growing assurance that, as King Solomon said, "He will direct our paths."

Decision-Making Principle #1: My level of trust must increase

"Trust in the Lord with all your heart…" (Pr. 3:5)

   – Trust increases when intimacy increases

   – Trust increases when visibility increases

   – Trust increases when unbelief decreases

Decision-Making Principle #2: Look at what I'm leaning on

"Trust in the Lord with all your heart… and do not lean on your own understanding." (Pr. 3:5)

   – Let humility temper your understanding

   – Do not be conformed to the world

Decision-Making Principle #3: Acknowledge God in all your ways

"Trust in the Lord with all your heart, and do not lean on your own understanding; in all your ways acknowledge him, and he will make straight your paths" (Pr. 3:5-6).

- Acknowledge him by creating a prayer buffer

- Acknowledge that he is the Lord of the Road

- Acknowledge him by learning to see what he is doing around you

Questions to Ponder

1. Why has God given human beings the unique ability to make decisions based on their free will to choose? What effect does our free will have on our relationship with God and on the direction of our lives?

2. Can you give some examples of how the phrase "I will pray over it" can sometimes be deceiving in the way that we make decisions?

3. If it is true that for God to direct our paths, we must trust him with all our heart, what are some of the ways that you struggle in really trusting God? How can you use the tools of intimacy, visibility, and turning from unbelief to increase your ability to fully trust him?

4. Can you give some examples of ways that you lean on your own understanding in the course of your life? How does humility and nonconformity with the world rebuild the support system that you find your security in?

5. Are there times when you struggle to acknowledge him in all your ways? Is there an upcoming decision in your life where you can acknowledge him by creating a prayer buffer, as well as remembering that he is the Lord of the Road?

Chapter Six

The Power of Consistency

One of the most common questions that I'm asked these days is, "How do you know that it's God speaking to you when you write down things in your journal?" Most people expect an exciting story for an answer, such as a vision or the words glowing on the pages of my journal. For many my answer is rather anti-climactic, "I know it's God based on the *consistency* of what I am hearing." In more than 30 years of journaling, I well know that I am able to write almost anything in my journal once, at any given time; but the words that I place my faith on (and make decisions based on) are the words I hear consistently time and time again. Consistency is not a very mesmerizing topic, for hearing something over and over again and can often seem pretty tedious, but I have found that hearing the same thing consistently creates an anchor for my faith that I can always depend on!

In the physical world we understand the power of consistency: For example, to learn a musical instrument I have to consistently play scales every day until I can find those notes without having to look for them or even think about them. To have a muscular body I have to consistently exercise and lift weights every day if my muscles are going to form into the shape that I want them to be. We understand that in the physical, nothing can take the place of consistency, but when it comes to areas in the spiritual world, we have a tendency to think that growth and maturity just somehow happen, by osmosis. I often tell people that hearing the voice of God is not a talent or even a gift, it is a skill! Any Christian who desires to hear God better must face the fact that it's going to take more than just wanting to hear him better, it's even going to take more than being ministered to in a Sunday service – Hearing God better requires that we develop the skill to consistently hear him when he speaks!

What is needed in our lives in order for us to be complete and lacking in nothing? Most of us would say that what is needed is great maturity or great power or perhaps greater knowledge and wisdom, but when the apostle James talked about completeness as a Christian, he saw it as the end result of only one thing… steadfastness! In James 1:4 (ESV), he said, "And let steadfastness have its full effect, that you may be perfect and complete lacking in nothing." The word being translated "steadfastness" is the Greek word *hypomone*, which is really two words put together, *hypo* the Greek word for "under" and *meno* the Greek word which means "to abide." In other words, completeness only comes when we are willing to consistently abide under him! Over the years, I've come to believe that the reason why people fail in their attempt to hear God more clearly is certainly not because God isn't speaking, but because they are unwilling to let steadfastness or consistency have its full effect! No matter how strong a Christian one may be, no amount of education or religious training can take the place of consistently sitting down every morning with the intention of developing the skill of taking dictation.

On the very last morning of the year 2011, I received a telephone call from my boss and friend, the founder of the Atlanta Vineyard, inviting me to come over to his house for coffee. As I sat down with him and his wife, we talked about the amazing victory that he had recently won over an incumbent mayor to become the new mayor of our small town in Georgia. He shared that even though, in the beginning, he felt that he could pastor the church as well as manage the city, he realized that he needed to step down after nearly 30 years of service. When he offered me the opportunity to lead the church,

I wasn't at all convinced that I could step into his shoes, but as is my habit, I took that weekend to go over my journal for 2011 – every page! As I highlighted everything that God had said to me that year about serving the Atlanta Vineyard, I was amazed at how consistently God had said that I was to be a part of transitioning the church into one that would be multiethnic and community-centered. Even though it was a big step of faith to accept that job, what's important to understand is that my faith was not based on my experience or whatever gifts or talents I might have, it was based on the *consistency* of what God had said in my journal for 2011.

Consistency has a way of building certainty as you are hearing over and over again words of direction or comfort from someone whom you trust. If we are not going to depend primarily on circumstances or feelings, then every Christian needs a way to be fairly certain that God is directing them on a certain path. I would propose that there is only one way to achieve that kind of certainty: by hearing God's instructions again and again and keeping a record of what he has said. It's common in some parts of the church to see this almost as a lack of faith. "God says it so I believe it" might be a good slogan, but it's very difficult to place your faith upon something you've only heard once. I often tell people that it's the highest expression of faith to ask God to repeat himself and to be determined to hear his word of direction again and again before acting on it. Of course, there does come a time when we have to trust him enough to obey, but he wants that trust to be firmly rooted in what he has said. We must never forget that Paul declared, "So then faith comes by hearing and hearing by the word of God" (Romans 10:17 NKJV).

Consistency also has a way of building habits in our lives (both good and bad). Habits and routines are important tools that enable us to really take hold of our inner lives and not be blown about by circumstances and situations. It's important to see taking dictation not as some kind of mystical experience but simply as one of the good routines every Christian needs in order to grow in their understanding of their relationship with God. One of the first things I do when mentoring people is to challenge them to buy a notebook and commit themselves to 10 minutes every morning for the next 30 days. In that short time, I ask them to look deeply at the Scripture and then write a sentence as to what God might be saying to them through that verse. Without exception, those who were willing to discipline themselves for 30 days found an amazing change in their ability to hear the voice of God. It wasn't that they were fasting or doing anything particularly spiritual, consistency alone had the power to draw them closer to God and to create a routine that would shape them for the rest of their lives.

Perhaps the most important thing to understand about consistency is that, above everything else, consistency is *abiding*. We saw earlier that the word steadfast means to "abide under," but now we should take a closer look at the word "abide" itself. When we read that word it's easy to think that it just means to stay close to him, but in many translations, it is interpreted to mean "to continue." When we substitute the word "continue" for the word abide it begins to give us a deeper understanding of the power of consistency.

Consistency Is the Key to Fruitfulness

(John 15:4 NKJV) "Abide in me, and I in you. As the branch cannot bear fruit by itself, unless it abides in the vine, neither can you, unless you abide in me."

If you substitute the word "continue" for the word abide you hear Jesus saying, "A branch cannot bear fruit by itself unless it continues to be connected in the vine." We understand this in agriculture, that fruitfulness is dependent on a consistent flow of nutrients through the vine and into the fruit. You can't graft and then remove a branch from the vine once a week and expect fruit to be produced! Yet this is exactly what we expect when it comes to our spiritual fruit and development as Christians. The plain truth is that if I'm not being consistent most mornings in giving him time to nourish me with words of comfort, encouragement, and direction then, by definition, I am not abiding in him!

It's not that God means for us to be slaves to some legalistic bondage in our efforts to take dictation, but we are bound to the way the kingdom works! Fruit requires a consistent flow of nutrients, and for believers, those nutrients are the words of God, spoken to our hearts. We must never forget that we are not servants who only have to await instructions from the master, we are part of the harvest that is growing in the world and if we do not consistently stay connected with our ears open, our generation could easily be one which will fail to produce fruit!

Consistency Enables Us to Ask

(John 15:7 NASB) "If you abide in me, and my words abide in you, ask whatever you wish, and it will be done for you."

We sometimes miss the "if/then" order that is in these words spoken by Jesus: he did not say "just ask whatever you wish, and I will do it for you." He said, "*If* you continue in me, and my words continue in you, *then* you will be in a position to ask and it will be done!" It's not that consistency earns the right to have our prayers answered, but that consistency in his word transforms us into being able to ask him for the things that he wants to answer! If you think about it, prayer itself is a very strange thing: we are asking an omnipotent being for something we want, as though he doesn't already know what we want. Yet the Apostle James clearly stated that, "You do not have because you do not ask God." (James 4:2) So apparently God chooses to wait until we ask, but notice that when you read the next verse in the Book of James, you find that there is a small caveat, "When you ask, you do not receive, because you ask with wrong motives" (James 4:3). Apparently, even though God waits until we ask, he also waits until we have grown up enough as Christians to know what to ask!

Everyone has experienced those times when we've asked God for something and it hasn't taken place in our lives. Sometimes it can be pretty devastating and causes us to wonder if God is listening or if is there some terrible secret sin in us that we're not aware of. Most people never consider the fact that God is waiting for us to abide in him to the point where we are mature enough to know what to ask. The Apostle John said it this way, "This is the confidence we have in approaching God: that if we ask anything according to his will, he hears us. And if we know that he hears us – whatever we ask – we know that we have what we asked of him" (I John 5:14-15). Asking according to his will is not just including the phrase "if it be thy will oh Lord" in your prayer, it is also about having an inkling of what his will is before I do the asking! I know that to many people, this sounds like a very strange way to pray but if you think about it, it's even stranger to think that prayer is activating God to do what we want or reminding God of those things that we need. Prayer is difficult to understand, but if we think of it as somewhat informed words (asking according to his will) spoken out in a way that mixes together with the purposes of God, we begin to see the reason for prayer: it is combining (in a small way) our words with the words of God to create changes in the world around us!

Consistency Builds Confidence

(I John 2:28 NASB) "And now, little children, abide in him, so that when he appears we may have confidence and not shrink back from him in shame at his coming."

While there are certainly many confident people in the world around us, a great majority of us struggle with this thing called confidence. With a lack of great talents or abilities, it is difficult to know just what I'm supposed to be confident in, but in order to really be a follower of Jesus we need the confidence to go when he says go. I find this statement in I John to be intriguing: that if we will abide (continue) in him, we will build in confidence to the degree that even when he comes again, we will not shrink back from him in shame! We sometimes read Scripture as though the only need for confidence is to face him at his second coming, but the real point of the verse is that continuing in him consistently builds up confidence every day between now and when he one day comes again.

For much of my early life, I was the least confident of people. In college I was shy, and I lived alone in a trailer off-campus. After dropping out of college I worked dead-end jobs that required no responsibility on my part: taking care of old folks as an orderly in a nursing home and working on an assembly line in a furniture factory. For me, confidence only started to grow in my life as I began to spend consistent time learning to listen to the words of God.

There is something about giving God time every morning to speak that creates a growing confidence in the one who is taking dictation. It's not a confidence based on always knowing everything, but knowing that when God desires to give direction, I have given him that time to speak. Following Jesus will always take us around many unexpected turns, but when I am consistently listening, I don't have to be afraid of the unexpected. I can be confident of what I've learned of the character of God and confident that he will guide me.

Consistency is the hallmark of a disciple

(John 8:31 ESV) "So Jesus said to the Jews who had believed him, 'If you abide in my word, you are truly my disciples.'"

What does it mean to be a disciple of Jesus? Is it only to name the name of Jesus, or perhaps to be an active church member or one who loves others and is generous to the poor? While all these things are important, it's interesting that Jesus declared to the Jews who had recently declared him Messiah, that the person who is truly his disciple is the one who abides (continues) in his word. It's important to note here that Jesus wasn't speaking of their salvation, which is a free gift and cannot be earned by any action, but was instead referring to those that he considered to be true disciples. The word being translated "disciple" in the Greek is the word *mathētēs* and it is the word that is used to describe a learner. Not the member of the church or the adherent of a particular creed or religion but one who has committed himself to learn from Jesus!

Almost all Christians, if asked, would say that they are disciples of Jesus, but, according to Jesus himself, if you are not consistently hearing his word, both in Scripture and in your heart, then it's going to be very difficult to be a learner. When Jesus was describing to his disciples what the Holy Spirit would be doing when he came upon the Earth, he said these words, "But when he, the Spirit of truth, comes, he will guide you into all the truth. He will not speak on his own; he will speak only what he hears, and he will tell you what is yet to come" (John 16:13). Notice that the Holy Spirit's work in making them disciples was not to help them become better students of the Torah or even to build a better religion, but to hear what the Holy Spirit was speaking to their hearts, that is the way God intended to guide them into all truth.

I've come to believe that there is a difference between a follower of Jesus and a disciple of Jesus: A follower has accepted God's way of salvation and been freed from his sins, but a disciple is one determined to never stop learning at the feet of Jesus! Becoming that second kind of person doesn't happen just because we want it to happen, it only happens when we are determined to be persistent and consistent in opening our hearts to hear the word of God. I've come to believe that the key to fruitful Christian growth is not some deep secret that only a few spiritual people know; in fact, it is the most obvious key to human existence – you have to be consistent if anything is going to develop in your life! I believe the apostle Paul was pointing to this when he said, "Exercise yourself toward godliness. For bodily exercise profits a little, but godliness is profitable for all things" (I Timothy 4:7–8 NKJV). Godliness (being closer to God and being transformed into the image of his Son) does not come with age or even with religiosity – it is the result of exercise! I feel that many believers in our modern Christian culture today need to take a hard look, not at how much they love Jesus, but at how much they are willing to exercise as disciples of Jesus. There is, of course, a legalistic way that people can approach this, but there is also an exercise that is born of love and a deep desire to hear God more clearly.

Questions to Ponder

1. How would hearing something a dozen times from God in your journal in the course of a month affect your walk with God?

2. What kinds of lifestyle choices keep you from letting steadfastness have its full effect in your life?

3. What is the connection between abiding (consistently continuing) in the Vine and being truly fruitful as a Christian?

4. How does abiding (consistently continuing) enable you to ask in the right way in your prayers?

5. How would hearing something a dozen times from God in your journal in the course of a month affect your confidence?

Chapter Seven

The Power of Accountability

At this point in the book, it would be understandable to see taking dictation as the most private and individual practice that a person could be involved in. And even though it does involve learning how to go into the secret room and close the door, there is also a very important element that is *corporate* in nature: the element of accountability. The dictionary defines the word accountable as: "to be subject to giving an account or having the obligation to report, explain or justify something." In our modern church culture, this is not a very popular concept; people push back against the idea of having an obligation to report or explain or justify something about themselves. While it is true that there is a form of obligation that is legalistic and is forced upon others, there is another kind of obligation, which is chosen voluntarily out of a desire to grow. It's described this way in Romans 15:1 (ESV), "We who are strong have an obligation to bear with the failings of the weak, and not to please ourselves." The word being translated "obligation" in the English Standard Version is the Greek word *opheilō* and it means "to owe someone something." Obligation is a concept that works both ways, if the strong are obliged to bear with the failings of the weak, then the weak are obliged to allow the strong to bear them up!

For many years I preached and taught about the importance of hearing God's voice on a daily basis but was frustrated to see so little real change in the lives of the people I was preaching to. The problem was not that people didn't see the importance of this idea, we would have altar calls and times of ministry as people responded to God's call to draw closer and to listen to his voice – but I only saw real results when I began to hold people to the obligation of accountability! About two years into my time as pastor of the Atlanta Vineyard, I decided to put on hold the different kinds of leadership schools that we had operated in the past and made the decision to start mentoring people one-on-one. This is probably the most time-consuming thing that a pastor can do, and it certainly gave me a full calendar every week, but I found that when I met with people on a weekly or biweekly basis and asked them to simply read to me from their journal, most started to immediately grow in their ability to take dictation.

One young woman in our church had immigrated with her family from South America when she was a teenager and after several years in the United States, she came to our church with a deep desire to know God more. After agreeing to an accountability relationship, she started to come to the church office every other week, reading from the journal that she had started keeping. As the months went by, I was amazed not only by the pages she started to fill in her prayer journal, but also the depth of what God was speaking to her. During that year of accountability, not only did God speak deep healing into her heart but he also clearly called her to the mission field, which resulted in a missions training school in the UK and outreach into Africa. Remembering the shy young woman that we met when she came to our church, I'm not sure that she could have found the strength to take that path if she had not encountered the power of accountability in taking dictation.

To understand the kingdom of God, we have to really take hold of the fact that everything in God's kingdom is done in and through relationships. Even Jesus from the very beginning was in an eternal relationship that we understand as Father, Son, and Holy Spirit: one God that exhibits the very character and nature of relationship within himself. All that God wants to do on Earth is done through relationships: from gathering people together to be a church family or sending them out to be incarnational in other cultures, it all involves people interacting with each other. But those relationships can never be fully formed if there is not a conscious decision to be accountable to one another. Let's take a closer look at the power of accountability to help us better develop the skill of hearing God's voice every day.

Accountability Fulfills the Law of Christ

(Galatians 6:2 ESV) "Bear one another's burdens, and so fulfill the law of Christ."

Accountability in the kingdom of God is not just holding each other accountable but holding *up* each other in an accountability relationship. There is a tendency in our modern church culture to only see "bearing each other's burdens" as helping someone bear up under the weight of tragedy or difficulty, but the burden of discipleship is also something that must be shared by all. Notice also the intriguing statement here: that when we are accountable to bear one another's burdens we are fulfilling the law of Christ, not the law of Moses but the law of Christ. What is this "law of Christ" that Paul is referring to? Most theologians believe that the law of Christ is the new commandment that Jesus gave us in John 13:34 where he said, "A new command I give you: Love one another. As I have loved you, so you must love one another." If this is indeed the law of Christ, then it's sobering to realize that the only way this can be fulfilled is not through sentimentality or shallow friendships but through bearing one another's burdens! Accountability is, of course, a much broader topic than just how it is used in taking dictation. When we begin to realize that it holds the key to following the new commandment Jesus has given us, it gives us a new motivation to be accountable as well as to hold others accountable to hear God's voice – the motivation of love!

When I bring someone into this most intimate process of hearing God's word, I'm not doing it in a way that is using them as a convenient tool to help me be consistent, I'm expressing the very essence of love: a willingness to be open and vulnerable to another person and to allow them to see into what God is saying to me in my inner room. When I agree to mentor another person by holding them accountable, I'm not trying to manipulate them into becoming like me, I'm expressing the only true measurement of love – sacrifice – by giving them time and working accountability sessions into my weekly schedule. And could it be that what causes love to grow cold in our modern church culture is not just the influence of the world around us, but our unwillingness to fulfill the law of Christ by bearing one another's burdens in accountability?

Accountability Is the Tool That Shapes Us

(Proverbs 27:17) "As iron sharpens iron, so one person sharpens another."

Notice that King Solomon understood that this sharpening and shaping process in our character is not something that God only does directly in our lives – it also requires the involvement of a person to sharpen another. After several years of mentoring people in the skill of taking dictation, I've noticed that there is a real difference in the clarity and even the quality of personal prayer journals when they've been kept only in the inner room and never shared with another person. When there's not another person to sharpen us, it's easy to let our journal become muddled and disorganized. Sometimes just the knowledge that we are going to read our journal entries to another person keeps us on point and helps us to concentrate more on what we feel the Lord is saying to our heart and through his word. My wife and I have read our journals to each other every morning for many years now and I've noticed that being accountable to one another in taking dictation has made several significant changes in the way we journal:

It Has Shaped Our Use of Time

People are sometimes wrongly impressed when they discover that for 25 years, my first hour has belonged to God. They are amazed at my self-discipline, but the truth is that my first hour belongs to God simply because my wife holds me accountable for how I spend that first hour (and I hold her accountable too). As a former hippie/musician/college dropout I was certainly not the epitome of a disciplined person, but the simple mutual agreement to hold each other to take dictation in our quiet times every morning has shaped the way I spend my day. Most people find it hard to organize themselves and many fall into the false belief that only "organized people" can accomplish that. But could it be that an accountability relationship, not just inner discipline, is the key to shaping our day in a way that gives more time to God?

It Has Shaped Our Confidence

One of the thrilling things about sharing journals together on a regular basis is that you discover God sometimes is saying the same thing to both of you. There have been many times over the years where God has not only led us to the same Scripture in our journal, but even said very similar things to each of us. The times that we have sought God's will over big decisions, it's been amazing how similar journal entries have built up a tremendous confidence in us to take a risk and to step into something new and challenging in our lives.

In 20+ years of pastoring people, I've become convinced that what keeps most people from answering God's call to go is not that they don't hear that call, but they don't have the confidence to believe that it's really coming from God. It's all too easy to make promises to oneself to follow through on what God was saying, filing that call away in the back of our minds with every intention of getting back to it, but gradually forgetting what God had said. I've always liked the imagery in Ecclesiastes 4:9-11 (ESV) where it says, "Two are better than one, because they have a good reward for their toil. For if they fall, one will lift up his fellow. But woe to him who is alone when he falls and has not another to lift him up! Again, if two lie together, they keep warm, but how can one keep warm alone?" There is a confidence that comes when there's two instead of one: the confidence that if I fall someone will lift me up; the confidence that when it gets cold on the journey, two lying together can keep warm. When two people hold each other accountable to take dictation there develops the confidence that when one is discouraged the other will lift him up, or when one grows cold and is not hearing God's voice, the other can encourage him with words from the Lord.

It Has Shaped Our Obedience

One of the somewhat uncomfortable things about taking dictation in a prayer journal is that sometimes God asks you to do something that you would really rather not do! It might be making something right with another person or speaking up when your opinion might not be appreciated by all. In the years that my wife and I have shared our journal with each other, there have been many occasions where she might remind me (or I remind her) that we haven't yet followed through on what God seemed to be instructing us to do.

At the beginning of 2016 as America was embroiled in one of the most contentious presidential elections in our nation's history,

I started to receive almost daily words of exhortation from the Lord in my journal about the candidates that were so strong (and controversial) that I was quite afraid to share them with anyone in the church except my accountability partners. My fear increased when, after a couple of months, I felt the Lord was instructing me to write a letter to my congregation about the responsibility we have to apply godly leadership principles to our leaders in the United States. I knew that it would be misinterpreted by some in our church (and it was) and I knew that some might leave the church (a few did) but what enabled me to finally obey and mail out the only political "letter from the pastor" that I've ever sent to a congregation was the power of accountability. I am the least political person that I know, so my obedience to what I felt God was instructing me to do was not sharpened by strong political opinions, but by my willingness to be accountable to my church council, as well as to my wife.

In Hebrews 10:24 (ESV) it says, "And let us consider how to stir up one another to love and good works" and that points to a very important truth of the kingdom: that things like obeying God to love others, and obeying him by following through with good works, need to be stirred up by another person. Taking dictation is a wonderful comfort and it strengthens us and directs us, but it also will always challenge us! Accountability to another person has a way of keeping things stirred up so that we don't allow God's instructions to become hardened and forgotten.

Accountability Creates Checks and Balances

(I John 4:1 ESV) "Beloved, do not believe every spirit, but test the spirits to see whether they are from God, for many false prophets have gone out into the world."

This verse points to one of the greatest fears that people have when it comes to trying to write down what God might be saying in a prayer journal: we can't believe every voice that whispers to us from the spiritual world; so how can we know, when prophesying to ourselves, that it is not false prophecy? John said that we should *test* it, using the word in the Greek *dokimazō*, which means "to recognize something as genuine after examination," and the best way to do that is in an accountability relationship! It's important to point out that using accountability as a system of checks and balances does not mean that someone examines your journal to see how logical it might be, but that someone is also praying and keeping a journal and is allowing the wisdom that God is giving them to temper the wisdom you feel that God is giving you. Accountability relationships provide checks and balances on a couple of different levels:

The Check and Balance Found In Scripture

I find it interesting that even the apostle Paul at the height of his influence and popularity still needed the check and balance of Scripture. When he spoke in the Jewish synagogue in the city of Berea, we are told: "Now the Berean Jews were of more noble character than those in Thessalonica, for they received the message with great eagerness and examined the Scriptures every day to see if what Paul said was true" (Acts 17:11). To me, this shows that we can receive a word from the Lord with eagerness and joy and still at the same time examine that word against Scripture to test its accuracy and truth. A lot of the strange doctrines that have come into the church over the years could probably have been avoided if that leader had been willing to be accountable to another person concerning what he felt God was saying to him.

Allowing another person to search the Scriptures in an accountability relationship does more than just protect us against false doctrine, it can also bring greater depth to what we feel God is saying. When we add similar passages to the one God is speaking to us that day, it gives a greater depth and balance to what God is saying through his Word. I've always found that hearing God's will being spoken through a different heart has always provided a balance to what I felt God was saying to mine.

The Check and Balance Found In Friendship

I've found in my life that the issue I face with my prayer journal is not always whether or not God has spoken, but instead, it is often what I should do (or not do) in response to what he has spoken. An accountability partner is not just a functional role someone plays in our lives, it is a relationship and a friendship! There are times when we need someone who knows our strengths and our weaknesses and our maturity to help us put into practice what God is saying. For me, the check and balance of friendship helps me to not rush into things that I feel God might be saying. Quite often my wife will say things like, "You've only heard that once in your journal, let's wait and let God repeat himself." For my wife, the check and balance of friendship helps her to believe that she can really do what God is challenging her to do. Quite often she hears me saying encouraging words that help her not to doubt herself or her abilities.

The Check And Balance of Mutual Submission

When we allow ourselves to be held accountable to another person, it is a form of submission. Paul said in Philippians 2:3, "Do nothing out of selfish ambition or vain conceit. Rather, in humility value others above yourselves." There is no better balance to ambition or conceit than being willing to choose to value another's opinion over your own. Having an accountability partner does not mean that someone controls your life, but that you are willing to really listen with an open and submissive heart to someone else's view. I have found that it's almost impossible for secret ambition to live long in my heart if I'm submitting to another in an accountability relationship.

In learning any new skill, the power of accountability must not be underestimated. A music student must be accountable to his music teacher if he is going to develop skill on his instrument; a pupil must be accountable to his teacher if he is going to increase his knowledge and ability. And the same is true in hearing God's voice: accountability gives us the power to be consistent and to learn good spiritual habits; it also gives us a valuable tool in sharpening that skill, as well as the protection provided by checks and balances. As Paul said to the Colossian Christians, "Let the word of Christ dwell in you richly, teaching and admonishing one another in all wisdom" (Colossians 3:16 ESV). God's word dwells most richly in us when we are admonishing one another!

Questions to Ponder

1. Why is it so difficult to be accountable to another person in our modern church culture?

2. If accountability is bearing one another's burdens, what happens to the law of Christ (love one another as Jesus has loved us) if you reject accountability? Give some examples of how not fulfilling the law of Christ explains many of the weaknesses of today's Christianity.

3. If accountability is a tool that shapes your prayer journal and your ability to hear God's voice, what happens to quiet times if your prayer journal stays hidden in your inner room?

4. If accountability provides checks and balances to your quiet times, what confusion can develop concerning the things that you feel you are hearing from God?

5. Would you be willing to find someone who is already keeping a prayer journal and talk to them about entering into an accountability relationship?

Chapter Eight

Becoming Sheep Again

What type of lifestyle enables a person to most effectively hear the voice of God? Is it the highly disciplined person who organizes every minute of the day? Is it the person who is separated from the world or perhaps the one who diligently studies the Bible? We've already seen that there are things that can hinder us from hearing God's voice: hardness of heart or the temptation to take shortcuts in our relationship with God. When it comes to a lifestyle best suited to hear God, Jesus said that it was the lifestyle of a sheep! In John 10: 2-3, he said, "The one who enters by the gate is the shepherd of the sheep. The gatekeeper opens the gate for him, and the sheep listen to his voice." Notice that he didn't say that the sheep in the flock get together each day to decide if they're going to listen to the shepherd's voice, but that being a sheep involves hearing the shepherd! Jesus referred to those who followed him as sheep a surprising number of times in the Gospels, even his last words to Peter were not "lead my church" but "feed my sheep" (John 21:17). When you look for sheep references in the Old Testament, you realize that God saw us as sheep long before the time of Jesus. David said in Psalm 79:13 (NKJV), "So we, your people and sheep of your pasture, will give You thanks forever" and in Psalm 23 he described the lifestyle of one who has embraced the Lord as his shepherd.

Sheep are not the most flattering animals to be associated with, they are helpless and domesticated and require constant oversight. They are not predators and, without the help of shepherds, can easily become prey. As a young Christian, I had the idea that the designation of "sheep" was temporary and that one day I would grow into something a little more fearsome, like a lion. In my later years, however, I've come to realize that in God's kingdom, it is the meek who will inherit the Earth, and an overcoming lifestyle can appear to the world as meek as a sheep following a shepherd!

So, what does it mean to be a sheep? In John chapter 10, for an amazing 16 verses, Jesus shared his thoughts about our relationship with him as sheep to Shepherd. It is perhaps the most detailed description in the New Testament of what it means to become a sheep, so let's look closely at part of it: (John 10:1 – 5) "Very truly I tell you Pharisees, anyone who does not enter the sheep pen by the gate, but climbs in by some other way, is a thief and a robber. The one who enters by the gate is the shepherd of the sheep. The gatekeeper opens the gate for him, and the sheep listen to his voice. He calls his own sheep by name and leads them out. When he has brought out all his own, he goes on ahead of them, and his sheep follow him because they know his voice. But they will never follow a stranger; in fact, they will run away from him because they do not recognize a stranger's voice." It is significant that Jesus was speaking these words to Pharisees, the religious leaders of Israel, and because they were religious leaders, Jesus was pointing out something that often occurs when people put their faith in religion instead of in God: they lose the relationship of a sheep to a shepherd. When you read through these words, it's amazing to see how much of this sheep-shepherd relationship depends upon speaking and hearing. Again and again, Jesus points out that the sheep aren't rounded up like cattle but led by the *voice* of a shepherd. So, let's unpack these words of Jesus and try to understand what it means to become sheep again.

Sheep Listen

(John 10:2-3) The one who enters by the gate is the shepherd of the sheep. The gatekeeper opens the gate for him, and the sheep listen to his voice…"

Perhaps it is the vulnerability of sheep that causes them to listen carefully to what's happening around them and to stay together in a protective flock, listening to the movements of their fellow sheep and to the warnings of their leader. It is because of these instincts that people who raise sheep understand that they can't be treated in the same way that you would treat a herd of horses, with bit and bridle. Perhaps this is what God was talking about through the psalmist when he said, in Psalm 32:8-9, "I will instruct you and teach you in the way you should go; I will counsel you with my loving eye on you. Do not be like the horse or the mule, which have no understanding but must be controlled by bit and bridle or they will not come to you." Even though God clearly said that he didn't want us to be like a horse or mule that must be controlled with a bit and bridle, that is exactly what we so often demand of God: that he stop us if we're wrong or turn us in the right direction, when all along, the desire of our Heavenly Father is to instruct us in the way that we should go!

If you think about it, to listen is a choice that we must make, it will not be forced upon us by over-riding our free will, we must decide that we want to listen to God. I've discovered that the more I see myself as a sheep, the greater the motivation I have to listen to the shepherd. I was much more self-confident twenty years ago than I am today, and like a sheep, I understand that I won't last very long at all without the guidance of the shepherd. There is a humility that comes with choosing to listen instead of going our own way, which is why the Bible points out that pride always leads to a fall. There is also a cost that comes with choosing to listen, the cost of setting aside time as well as the cost of laying down your own words and allowing God to enter the conversation. Jesus didn't say that his sheep had to be tied up before they would listen, he said that there was something in the very nature of his sheep that wanted to hear his voice!

Sheep Have Names

(John 10:3) "He calls his own sheep by name and leads them out."

When Jesus said that, he was pointing to a principle of following him that is easy to overlook: he didn't say that the shepherd stands behind the sheep and waves his staff and drives them out, but that he calls them by name and leads them out! Although it sounds rather quaint that a shepherd in the old days would have names for his sheep and would be able to tell one sheep from another, it is also an illustration that gives us rich insight into the kind of relationship God wants to have with us. Later in his sixteen-verse "sheep discourse" Jesus touches on this idea again when he says in John 10:14-15, "I am the good shepherd; I know my sheep and my sheep know me, just as the father knows me and I know the Father." In the culture of the New Testament, a name was something more than just a title created by a baby's parents, names spoke of the character of a person and his family's traditions and values. God would even rename people (like Peter and Abram) to better reflect who they really were, and when Jesus said that the shepherd calls his own sheep by name, he was saying that there is meant to be a deep knowledge between the sheep and the shepherd. This knowledge was so deep that in the following verse, Jesus actually said that he knows his sheep (and they know him) in *the same way* that the Father knows Jesus, and Jesus the Father – and what way is that exactly? Not the way of a Lord and his servant, but the way of a Father and his Son!

One of the advantages of getting older is that you have a longer period of life to be able to look back on and to learn from, and when I look back on my life it was definitely this revelation, that Jesus wants me to know God in the same way that he knows the Father, that was a turning point in my development as a Christian. As I mentioned earlier in the book, up until that point my relationship with God was mostly a "Lord-relationship" where I declared him

Lord of my life and I was willing to do whatever he wanted me to do. But there came a time while serving in the Philippines that I decided to carefully read through the book of John several times, and as I meditated on the story of Jesus, I realized that there was a "thread" running through that story that tied together so much about Jesus: that his relationship with the Father was so intertwined and dependent that if you could somehow remove that relationship, *you would have almost nothing left of Jesus!* You would have no miracles, because Jesus said the Son can only do what he sees the Father doing. You would have no preaching, because Jesus proclaimed that the word he was speaking were the words of the Father. You wouldn't even have his personality and character, because Jesus said when you looked at him you were looking at the Father. The revelation for me was that God really does know my name in the way that a Father knows the name of his child, and that he wants me to know his name and his voice in the same way that a sheep knows the voice of the shepherd.

Along with that revelation also came the realization that, with a few years' experience under my belt in the Philippines, you could remove my own relationship with God and things would not change all that much: I had learned to preach and I had learned to build a team and how to run a medical clinic. It was very much a "sheep moment" when I saw that I was not nearly as dependent on God as Jesus had been, and that marked the time when I began to put more effort into knowing God and hearing his voice than I did into becoming a better pastor.

A Kingdom of Sheep

(John 10:16) "I have other sheep that are not of this sheep pen. I must bring them also. They too will listen to my voice, and there shall be one flock and one shepherd."

In the final verse of the "sheep discourse" that Jesus gives us in the 10th chapter of John, we are now shown a much wider view of what it means to become sheep: He points out that there are other sheep who were not in that particular Jewish sheep pen and that they too will, not embrace a new religion, but listen to his voice. And then Jesus gives an amazing description of the kingdom of God, a place where there is "one flock and one shepherd." Sometimes it's hard to define the kingdom of God: is it one people living under the same rules? Or perhaps it is one people who have the same theology? But could it be that in God's eyes the kingdom of God is one flock listening to one shepherd! He seemed to be pointing to this in Luke 12:32 (ESV) when he said to his followers, "Fear not little flock, for it is your Father's good pleasure to give you the kingdom." I used to read that as though Jesus were saying, "Despite the fact that you are pitiful sheep, the Father will still give you the kingdom" but now I have come to believe that what he meant was, "Because you are sheep, I will give you my kingdom!" Could it be that taking dictation, learning to hear the voice of the shepherd and keep a record of what he has said, is much more than just a new way to have a quiet time? What if hearing God's voice was one of the ways that he uses to bind Christians together into one flock; to have this in common despite our differences in theology and practice? At the risk of sounding radical, I believe that taking dictation, hearing God's voice, will be the glue that binds believers together in the future. Let's look at a few reasons why it is sheep, hearing the voice of the shepherd, who build his kingdom.

The Kingdom of God Is Not a Geographical Place

One of the first things that the Pharisees asked when they realized that Jesus claimed to be the Messiah was, "When will the kingdom of God come?" His answer was intriguing. In Luke 17:20–21 (GNB), he said: *The Kingdom of God does not come in such a way as to be seen.*

No one will say, 'Look, here it is!' or, 'There it is!'; because the Kingdom of God is within you." Some translations interpret that sentence as "the kingdom of God is in your midst" and the Greek can go either way. but what if the coming kingdom was not something that could be seen on the outside, but something happening to a believer on the inside? Christians for centuries have prayed that part of the Lord's Prayer that says, "Your kingdom come," and then wondered if they would ever see it come in their lifetime, but what if it has come already in the hearts of those determined to be a sheep and to grow in their ability to hear his voice?

The Kingdom of God Is Not a Religion

A simple definition of religion might be: "man's attempts to get closer to God." That definition applies not only to the world's religions but even the Christian religion. But a simple definition of the kingdom of God might be: "God's desire to get closer to man." Perhaps this is why you don't find Jesus teaching his followers the steps needed to be acceptable to God, for he understood that it was the cross that would bring reconciliation, not the religious works of people. When you think about it, taking dictation is in many ways the opposite of religion: it is believing that God can talk to me one-on-one and there is no need for an intermediary or a system to interpret what he is saying. Even though we need the accountability that comes from gathering together as his church, the kingdom itself is not a particular church but a flock in one sheep pen, as well as a flock in another pen, all hearing the same voice of the shepherd.

The Kingdom Looks Like the Shepherd

The Apostle John understood this when he said in John 1:3, "Through him all things were made; without him nothing was made that has been made." Notice that everything God created in the beginning was not created along with Jesus, but *through* him. This means that every part of the kingdom of God has passed through the heart and character of Jesus and resembles him in every way. He is the Good Shepherd, and it is impossible to be a fruitful part of the shepherd's kingdom if we are not willing to be kingdom people who are effective sheep. One of the best descriptions of what it means to be an effective sheep of the Good Shepherd is in the first three verses of Psalm 23 where it says: "The Lord is my shepherd; I shall not want. He makes me lie down in green pastures. He leads me beside still waters. He restores my soul. He leads me in paths of righteousness for his name's sake" (Psalm 23:1–3 ESV). Notice that the definition of an effective sheep is not what the sheep does for the shepherd, but what the sheep allows the shepherd to do for him. A kingdom of sheep are people who are willing to let the Lord teach them how to lie down in green pastures and depend upon him more than they depend upon their own works. A kingdom of sheep are people who are willing to be led by the voice of the shepherd beside still waters and on the path of righteousness.

Being kingdom people in the shepherd's kingdom also goes beyond just learning to be well-trained sheep, for in the kingdom of God our ultimate role is to be transformed into an image of the Shepherd himself! In II Corinthians 3:18 the apostle Paul said it this way: "And we all, who with unveiled faces contemplate the Lord's glory, are being transformed into his image with ever-increasing glory, which comes from the Lord, who is the Spirit." And this truth is probably the most important reason why we must learn to listen to his voice and behold his glory daily: that we might be a kingdom people who resemble the King himself. One of the things that I am learning as I make my home in a new country in my mid-60s is that what people need to see is not competing religions but the heart and the character of Jesus in me! And even though that sounds very simplistic, as an experienced former pastor I find it to be very challenging. It means that I cannot rely on the way that I might have built a church in Russia or the way I might have reached the poor in the Philippines, but that I must be willing in a much greater way, to let God speak through me and shine his presence through me and lead me in the way that only a shepherd can lead.

Learning to take dictation can never be accomplished through just a systematic and disciplined effort to keep a prayer journal or meditate on God's Word, I believe that it also requires a radical change of lifestyle and a willingness to embrace vulnerability and meekness and dependency just as sheep must do. This kind of lifestyle flies in the face of the militaristic view of Christianity, but, in my opinion, it is essential if we want to learn to really hear the voice of God. Someone once said that, in the end, everyone has about as much of God as they really want, and many are satisfied with the relationship of horse and rider, expecting to be controlled by bit and bridle, but in God's heart there is the desire for a much greater relationship: the kingdom of sheep who are united in their desire to follow the voice of the Shepherd.

Questions to Ponder

1. What keeps you from really embracing the lifestyle of a sheep?

2. If to be a sheep is to be a creature that carefully listens to the shepherd, how would you rate your ability to hear his voice? Are you more of a horse (or mule) that needs a bit and bridle?

3. Do you believe that God knows your name in the deeper biblical sense (your innermost character)? What is keeping you from having the same dependent relationship that Jesus had?

4. How does Jesus' description of one flock and one shepherd change your understanding of how the Kingdom grows and develops?

5. Ask yourself honestly, "Am I ashamed to be seen as a sheep?" What are some ways that I can develop the philosophy that His strength is made perfect in weakness?

Chapter Nine

Changing Our Thinking

How can one know the perfect will of God? In this book, I've tried to make the point that a big part of knowing God's will is learning to hear his voice on a regular basis and keep a record of what you feel he might be saying. And while I do believe that taking dictation is an important skill in learning to hear his voice, I also believe that taking dictation does more than just give us information about ourselves and about our calling.

When the apostle Paul took up the subject of how someone can know God's perfect will, he said something very important in the 12th chapter of Romans, "Don't copy the behavior and customs of this world, but let God transform you into a new person by changing the way you think. Then you will learn to know God's will for you, which is good and pleasing and perfect" (Romans 12:2 NLT). Notice in this verse that in order to reach the goal of knowing God's perfect will, two things must be accomplished in our lives: 1) We must be determined not to copy the behavior and the customs of the world, and 2) We must allow God to transform us by changing the way we think. And in the NIV version, the promise is, "Then you will be able to test and approve what God's will is – his good, pleasing and perfect will" (Romans 12:2). That is a very big promise! If God really means what he has promised, then it should be the main task of every Christian to understand how to not conform to the ways of the world but to be transformed in the way that we think. Let's take this verse apart and try to understand how to reach the promised goal of being able to test and approve what God's perfect will really is.

Looking At Vs. Looking Along The Word of God

"Don't copy the behavior and customs of this world…" (Romans 12:2)

In an essay by C.S. Lewis, entitled *Meditation in a Toolshed* that was originally published in *The Coventry Evening Telegraph* in 1945[4] and later reprinted in a collection of essays called *God in the Dock*, C.S. Lewis pointed out that there are two very different ways that we look at things. In the essay, he said:

"I was standing today in the dark toolshed. The sun was shining outside and through the crack at the top of the door there came a sunbeam. From where I stood that beam of light, with the specks of dust floating in it, was the most striking thing in the place. Everything else was almost pitch-black. I was seeing the beam, not seeing things by it. Then I moved, so that the beam fell on my eyes. Instantly the whole previous picture vanished. I saw no toolshed, and (above all) no beam. Instead I saw, framed in the irregular cranny at the top of the door, green leaves moving on the branches of a tree outside and beyond that, 90 odd million miles away, the sun. Looking along the beam and looking at the beam are very different experiences."

So often the ways and the customs of the world are to look only at the beam of light itself, as Lewis did; to analyze something and seek to only understand the mechanism by which it works. But as most people know, there is a great difference between observing an experience and having an experience! A scientist might be able to accurately describe the way that hormones and pheromones work to create the feelings one calls love, but they might still have absolutely

---

4 Lewis, C.S. (1945). "Meditation in a Toolshed." *The Coventry Evening Telegraph*. Retrieved in Jan. 2020 from: ktf.cuni.cz/~linhb7ak/Meditation-in-a-Toolshed.pdf

no understanding of how love completely changes the way one sees the world.

In the same way, it's easy for Christians to conform to the ways of the world in the way that one looks at the Word of God: analyzing it and studying its contextual meaning but never looking along the "light beam" of God's Word. We see the word (which is not a bad thing) but we are not seeing things by means of the Word of God. There in the toolshed, when C.S. Lewis stepped into that beam of light and looked along that beam, he could not only see, in that narrow shaft of light, the colors and the leaves outside the toolshed, he could even see the sun 90 million miles away! Looking at the beam and looking along the beam were two very different experiences.

In my 40+ years of hanging around with Christian leaders, I've often wondered why it is that someone can have such a deep knowledge of the Word of God, memorizing great portions of the Bible and having fluency in Hebrew and Greek, and yet they often seem to still rely on knowing God's will the way that a baby Christian would know his will: looking only to circumstances or feelings. Perhaps the revelation that Lewis had in the toolshed points to one answer to this anomaly: looking at the word and looking at things through the word are two very different experiences.

So how does taking dictation help us to look "along the beam" of the Word of God? Whatever the process might be, we can tell from our text in Romans that it has to be the *opposite* of the behavior and customs of the world. Again, there's nothing wrong with looking *at* the beam of light that is the Word of God: we need to have a deep understanding of the content and the context of the Word, but if we are going to learn how to look along that beam that illuminates the heart and character of God, we need to understand the differences.

The Difference Between Questioning and Being Questioned

Most people, when they begin to read the Bible, see it primarily as a book of answers for many of their questions about God and the human race. To find those answers you have to analyze what the Word of God is actually saying and develop a theology anchored in the Word. But there is also something else that must happen in our Bible reading if we are going to no longer conform to the ways of the world – to move from having questions for the Bible to letting the Bible question us!

I discovered in Russia back in the 90s during my meetings with Professor Peacmonik that it was possible for a person to have a deep knowledge of the content of the Word of God and yet have no conception of the heart and character of God. He even told me once, "I'm not a Christian, I'm a scientist," and it was clear that despite all of the questions that he studied in the Bible, he had never allowed the Bible to question him.

One step towards transitioning from "looking at" to "looking along" is not being afraid to let that beam fall upon our eyes and ask, "What is this verse saying to me?" It's not always comfortable being questioned by the written Word of God or by the still small voice in our hearts, but when we allow God's voice to be living and active and sharper than any two-edged sword; when we are willing to let the voice of God judge the thoughts and the intents of our heart, then we have started looking along the word, not just at the word of God.

The Difference Between Seeing and Being Illuminated

As much as I love the illustration of the light beam in the toolshed, there is another side to that illustration that Lewis doesn't mention in his essay: not only did that beam of light allow him to look along its path to see what was outside the toolshed, it also illuminated to some degree the man standing in the toolshed. If I had been standing with him that day in that dark building, I would probably have seen his face as he allowed the beam to fall upon his eye – for the consequence of looking along that beam is to bring into the light what was previously in darkness!

This truth points to another difference between "looking at" something and "looking along" something. When we are conforming to the ways of the world and only looking at a truth in an analytical way, we are, in a sense, stepping away from that truth in order to see its context and its overall meaning. While this is needed in order to have greater knowledge about God's Word to us, it is a very different experience from allowing God's Word to light up our lives in what can sometimes be a sharp and even merciless spotlight. One of the interesting things about the coming of Jesus has to do with the way people reacted when light invaded darkness. In John 3:19 (NKJV), Jesus said, "And this is the condemnation, that the light has come into the world, and men loved darkness rather than light..." There is something in all of us that would prefer certain things to remain hidden in darkness and human beings have a remarkable talent in justifying why it's better to keep those things in darkness. Looking at my own life, I can see how tempting it can be to only look at the beam. Because I am a teacher of the Word, it's easy to substitute "looking at" activities in the place of "looking along" activities in my quiet times with God. But I learned some years ago, that the ultimate cost of knowing God better is, in his illuminating light, that people will know *me* better.

For many years in my Christian experience, I interpreted the phrase, "Jesus is the light of the world" to mean only that his teaching would light the path of the human race towards peace and righteousness, but Jesus had a much broader view of what it meant to be the light of the world. In the Book of John, he said, "I am the world's light. No one who follows me stumbles around in the darkness. I provide plenty of light to live in" (John 1:8 The Message). If we are going to move beyond just looking at God's words, we must embrace the fact that it means a willingness to live in the light of that word; for ultimately, he is light and "in him there is no darkness at all" (1 John 1:5).

The Difference Between Knowing and Loving

I've always found it interesting that, in the midst of a roaring controversy concerning whether or not Christians should eat meat offered to idols, Paul pointed out that just looking at what the Old Testament Scriptures said about this would not actually build up the church. In I Corinthians 8:1, he said, "Now about food sacrificed to idols: We know that we all possess knowledge. But knowledge puffs up while love builds up." In other words, we have all looked at what the law says, but only looking at something puts one in danger of a very specific condition – being puffed up by knowledge! The Greek word that is being translated as "puffs up" is the word *physio* whose literal meaning is "to inflate." Most people believe that he is using this phrase metaphorically by referring to how knowledge can make someone proud, but it is also true that knowledge alone (looking at the beam and not along the beam) can be inflated in our churches to the point where there is room for almost nothing else! It's so easy to read that verse as though Paul is saying, "Knowledge builds up and love will build up even more," but what he is saying is that knowledge can give the appearance of something that is growing, but only love can truly build people up into what God intends them to be. If we continue his thought, he goes on to say, "But knowledge puffs up while love builds up. Those who think they know something do not yet know as they ought to know. But whoever loves God is known by God" (I Corinthians 8:1-3). In other words, when we look at the Word, we may think we know all there is to know, but when we look along the Word of God, we discover our love for God and a greater intimacy with God. Again, a scientist can know all there is to know about the chemistry of love, but he must himself step into the stream of what it means to love before he will fully know the reality of that word.

Let's now go back to our foundational Scripture for this chapter and see the second important thing that Paul is saying about knowing the perfect will of God. "Don't copy the behavior and customs of this world, but let God transform you into a new person by changing the way you think. Then you will learn to know God's will for you, which is good and pleasing and perfect" (Romans 12:2 NLT).

Transforming The Way We Think

"...but let God transform you into a new person by changing the way you think."

Every Christian wants to be transformed into a new person who can better know the will of God, but the confusion comes in trying to understand *how* this transformation takes place. It is true that when we come to the cross and choose to be a Jesus-follower there is a transformation in our relationship with God: at that moment we are reconciled unto him. But most people notice that, in a lot of ways, we haven't really changed it all. Some people take hold of the "I'm just a sinner saved by grace" philosophy and don't expect to be a new person until they go to heaven. Others take hold of the "work out your own salvation with fear and trembling" philosophy and try to change themselves into a new person through self-discipline or religious practices.

I find it fascinating that Paul says in the book of Romans that God changes us into a new person by changing the way we think! He's not saying that God wants us to turn off our thinking or to restrict the ability of our mind to question and ponder, but to simply change the basic way our thought processes occur. And our text seems to infer that it is this transformation in the way we think that enables us to know the perfect will of God. Perhaps this was what Paul was referring to in his letter to the Ephesians when he said, "You were taught, with regard to your former way of life, to put off your old self which is being corrupted by its deceitful desires; to be made new in the attitude of your minds; and to put on the new self, created to be like God in true righteousness and holiness" (Ephesians 4:22–24). Notice that Paul seems to be implying that there is an important step between putting off the old self and putting on the new self: The step of being made new in the attitude of your mind! In my own journal recently, I felt that God was saying this to me concerning that text:

"People don't realize that it's impossible to put on the new self without first being made new in the attitude of your mind. You can't force yourself to think differently but you can, by yielding every day to my thoughts, allow me to transform the way that you think. Many Christians are "stuck" between the old self and the new self: they have turned from the old life, but their thinking is still conformed to the ways of the world. Only when their thoughts change will they be able to truly put on the new garments that I have created for them." – December 5, 2019.

As I pondered these words that I felt were from God that morning, I was struck by the image of Christians who are fully saved and completely reconciled to God through Jesus Christ – but who are still stuck between the old and the new! When I look back to my own early years as a Christian, it took me a long time to know God's will for my life. I was active in church and I loved God with all my heart, but for years I had no idea of what his perfect will might be. Looking back, I believe that I was one of those people stuck between the old and the new because the attitude of my mind had not been transformed. It's interesting that the word being translated as "attitude" in the Greek is the word *pneuma*, which is usually translated as "spirit" but the literal meaning of *pneuma* is "wind." I believe this points to one way of understanding how God wants to transform our thinking.

Thinking Changes When the Wind Changes

I've always loved the fact that when God transformed Adam from a lump of clay into a living being, he didn't snap his fingers; he blew the breath of life into Adam. In the natural, when we speak, we are moving air over our vocal cords and our words are carried forth upon that breath. Even though God doesn't speak in the same physiological way that we do, it is speaking just the same, and with his words there is that breath of the spirit that blows across our minds. It presents an interesting picture when you realize that Paul wasn't saying "change your attitude" but rather to let a renewed spirit from the breath of God blow into your thoughts and understanding.

Every sailor understands that you can't just sit in your sailboat and wait for the wind to come in your direction, you have to come into the wind instead. You must adjust the sail until you find the right angle in which the wind is blowing and only then will your boat move forward! I have always believed that we live in a world where God is always speaking, the breath of his thoughts never ceases to blow across the human race. David said in Psalm 139:17-18, "How precious to me are your thoughts, God! How vast is the sum of them! Were I to count them, they would outnumber the grains of sand." When you think of the trillions of grains of sand that are, for example, just on the beach along the Indian Ocean where I live, you realize that the sum total of thoughts that God had toward David, just one human being, was so vast in number that at the very minimum he was thinking of David every second of every minute of every hour of every day of David's life! It's true that the Psalms were written to be poetry, but even poetry can convey a truth: that over every individual human being there is a continuous flow of thoughts towards us, a wind that is blowing every second of every minute of every hour of our lives! Part of taking dictation in our quiet time is determining to learn how to "come into the wind" that we might hear those words and be renewed by the breath that's speaking those words.

Thinking Changes When We Change Our Mind

Even though many Christians acknowledge that there needs to be a change in the way they think about certain things, there is a tendency to be rather passive in the way that we expect that change to happen. We expect God to override our thought patterns or to just wake up one morning thinking differently, but the one immutable fact about transformation is that God will not violate the free will of a human being. He will not change our thoughts unless we are willing to change our minds! What causes a person to change his mind? In the natural, we change our minds when we've been presented with enough proof that something is different than we thought. We might change our minds if someone demonstrates to us that their character and intentions are much different than we thought they were. We sometimes change our mind simply when we realize that we were mistaken; that we've grown to see the world differently than we saw it in our younger days.

I have discovered one of the great benefits of taking dictation in my quiet time is that slowly I amass the evidence that I need in order to change my mind. For the first decade of my life as an adult, I fully believed that the only thing I had to offer the Kingdom of God was music, but after consistently hearing God say something different, morning after morning, I found that I was able to change my mind about what my contributions could be and began to believe that I could be a teacher and a pastor. In my second decade of adult life, I only thought of myself as an active layman in church, teaching Sunday school and leading children's church, but gradually in my journal, God began to convince me that he had called me to the mission field, and after a lot of convincing, I was able to think differently concerning my contribution to the nations. I don't believe that my thinking concerning myself and my abilities would have ever changed if I had not had many dozens of journal entries proving to me who I really was and what God could do with my life.

We really don't understand today the fundamental importance of changing our minds. When Jesus began his public ministry from town to town his primary message was, "Repent, for the kingdom of heaven has come near" (Matthew 4:17). We have a tendency to read that statement as though he were saying "turn from your sin" but the word repentance has a much deeper meaning than that. In the Greek, it's the word *metanoeō* which is made up of two primary words: *meta* which means to change, and *noeo* which means "your perception." Literally, Jesus was proclaiming in every place he went that you must change your mind because the kingdom of heaven has come near! It's so easy to relegate repentance to something that you did when you first came to Jesus, but the truth is that repentance (changing your mind) is the prerequisite for every new stage of growth in the development of God's Kingdom. I had to repent of trusting only in my musical ability before I could ever be a teacher and I had to repent of my limited view of what I could do before I could ever go to the nations. But that change of mind didn't just happen as I passively waited for change to happen, It happened because I was willing to let God, in my journal, convince me with a mountain of proof that what he saw was different than the way I saw things.

Thinking Changes When We Change Our Perspective

As a child of the 60s who grew up in the deep South, I am living proof that our thinking is very much influenced by our perspective.

Up until my senior year in high school, I went to segregated classes and the only black person that I had ever met was the maid who came to our modest rental home to clean three times a week. As in so many Southern families, she was (in my child's eyes) a part of my family and she certainly disciplined us kids as though she considered herself a part of our family! But there is no denying that my perspective as a white Southerner in the 60s was most definitely a deeply racist perspective. On the day that Martin Luther King Jr. was assassinated, I happened to be in my junior high school band practice when the announcement was made – and in one voice we all cheered as though some wonderful event had taken place (with no correction from our teachers). My parents and my relatives certainly considered themselves to be good (and even Christian) people; they were well-educated middle-class Americans who were upwardly mobile, but their thinking was molded by the racist bubble we all lived in. It was only when I went away to college, which presented a very different perspective on the world, that my thinking began to change. I experienced another radical change in perspective when I became a Jesus-follower at the age of 23 after hitchhiking across America from Alabama to Northern California. With that change, came a whole new way of thinking about people which motivated me to go out into the streets every evening with the other "Jesus Freaks" to give out tracts and share the Gospel. My perspective changed again when I launched out into the mission field of the Philippines in my early 30s, planting a church as well as a neighborhood healthcare center in the slums of Manila, which radically changed my thinking once more about the poor and about social justice in the world.

If we believe the central text for this chapter in Romans 12:2 (NLT) where Paul said, "let God transform you into a new person by changing the way you think. Then you will know God's will for you..." then we must understand that one of the major ways that God changes the way we think is by changing our perspective of the world around us. I believe that the greatest attack against the human race in the 21st century is not terrorism or communism but the way the enemy has used media to lock people into a rigid perspective that keeps them from changing the way they think. In our world today most people live in "silos" where their perspective is strengthened by people who see the world in the same way: conservatives watch Fox News and liberals watch CNN, chat rooms and Facebook pages are mostly composed of like-minded people. We must realize that if knowing God's will depends upon changing the way we think, then our society is systematically drawing us further and further away from his will by armoring our minds against any change of perspective.

Of course, the difficulty comes in asking the question: What kind of change should occur in our perspective in order to change our thinking? Conservative Christians would answer that question in one way and liberal Christians would answer that question in a different way, but the Bible gives a unique answer in trying to understand how to embrace a Kingdom perspective that alters our thinking. In Colossians 3:1-2 (ESV), it says, "If then you have been raised with Christ, seek the things that are above, where Christ is, seated at the right hand of God. Set your minds on things that are above, not on things that are on earth." Notice that our perspective is supposed to be determined not by where my political party is or where my home or church is – but by where Christ is! Where *he is* determines how we are to seek him, and that understanding will always bring a radical transformation in our perspective. I like the way that Eugene Peterson paraphrases these two verses in *The Message*, "So if you're serious about living this new resurrection life with Christ, act like it. Pursue the things over which Christ presides. Don't shuffle along, eyes to the ground, absorbed with the things right in front of you. Look up and be alert to what is going on around Christ—that's where the action is. See things from his perspective" (Colossians 3:1-2, *The Message*). If the church in the 21st-century is going to be a Christ-centered church, then we must truly understand that our perspective must not be centered on what our doctrinal statement is or what the current state of our culture is, but where Christ is!

So, where exactly is he? He has risen to a place of purity and holiness, so to change my perspective and seek him where he is means that I must value purity: remembering to turn my thoughts to whatever is true and whatever is honorable and whatever is just and whatever is pure and lovely and commendable (paraphrased from Philippians 4:8). He has risen to the ultimate center of all authority: the right hand of God the Father. Because this is where he is, it requires a change in my thinking about the authority that I have in the name of Jesus and the power of good to overcome evil. Because he has risen to a place that seems to be continually filled with the praises of God, it requires that I seek him in daily personal worship, allowing my perspective to change as I love him and adore him.

Christians who expect God to override their own will in order to show them his will are going to be greatly disappointed in their walk with God. Knowing his will is directly related to our willingness to submit to his will through learning how to not just look at the word of God but along the word of God; allowing him to change the way we think as we come into the wind of the breath of his voice each morning and change our perspective of what it means to be kingdom people.

Questions to Ponder

1. Can you look at your own personal quiet time and describe the difference between looking at the Word of God and looking along the Word of God?

2. What is happening when you allow the written Word of God to question you?

3. Why did the apostle Paul say that that you must be made new in the attitude of your mind before you can put on the new self?

4. What are some of the practical ways that you can "come into the wind" of the Spirit of God by opening your ears to hear the Word of God?

5. What determines the perspective that you have on life? Are there ways that you can allow Jesus to be more at the center of how you see the world?

Chapter Ten

Dealing with Surprises

A couple of years after starting our church in Perm, Russia, we found ourselves in the midst of an exciting time: the numbers were increasing in our church and we were just finishing our first full-time leadership training school. For about a year we had been holding services in the Mir (Russian for "peace") Theater, which was an old Soviet-era movie house complete with stage and tiered theater-style seating. Perm was rapidly changing, and younger Russians had no interest in going to the movies in such a stuffy old-fashioned place, but it was perfect for us! During that year, I began to hear in my journal that God wanted us to purchase the Mir Theater and after numerous entries, I started a fundraising campaign with our supporters and even sat down with the managers (it was still owned by the state) and made an offer. The city seemed anxious at first to get the old eyesore off its hands, but after several delays, we noticed that the land behind our building was being cleared, although no one knew why. After a couple more months, we discovered the reason: the very first Western-style shopping mall in Perm was going to be built right on that spot! When I discovered that we would not only be unable to purchase the theater, but would also have to move soon, I found myself sitting down and looking at my journal entries wondering, "What the heck happened?"

Perhaps it is this, more than anything else, that discourages people who begin to try to keep a record of what God is saying in their quiet times: when there is a surprise and things work out very differently than what you felt God had promised you! Some very uncomfortable questions can begin to arise during these times, "Have I just been deluding myself in writing down these words from God?" Or worse, "If God knew this disaster was going to happen, why did he tell me to go forward?"

I heard a story of a young woman who since high school had heard God's call to the mission field. She went to Bible school and there she met a young man who had the same call in his heart and they began to pray about marriage. She sought God on a regular basis and submitted their relationship to her pastor and felt convinced that God was telling her to marry. After their marriage, they attended a missions training school and towards the end of that school, she was shocked to discover that he had been involved in a relationship with another student. He repented and they continued their training, only for him to be unfaithful a second and even a third time. As she sat down in the office of her pastor, she asked a question that is a very hard one to answer, "If God knows everything then he knew that my husband would be unfaithful, so why did he clearly tell me to marry him? Great joke, God!" How would you counsel that young woman? It's possible, I suppose, that despite all of her effort she might not have heard God, and some might tell her that suffering through a divorce was part of God's plan for her life – but is there a different way to understand the surprises?

That young woman's theology of God (and the future) is a view shared by much of the Body of Christ: that if God is perfect and cannot be improved or diminished, then all that he has created cannot be changed or altered; it is predestined. This philosophy actually predates Christianity but was canonized through such people as St. Augustine and eventually morphed into two theological schools of thought: since God is perfect and cannot change, all of reality is preordained and either settled in God's will (Calvinism) or at least in God's knowledge (Arminianism). But is there an alternative perspective of the sovereignty of God?

I believe that it's helpful to view "surprises" in the context of the fact that even though God is unchangeable in the defining attributes of his character – his love and his faithfulness and his goodness – he is flexible in his plans and interactions with those free-will beings he has created. There are quite a few places in the Word of God where we see this flexibility: such as, for example, when he indicated that he could change his mind in the book of Jeremiah saying, "If that nation against which I have spoken turns from its evil, I will relent and reverse my decision concerning the devastation that I intended to do" (Jeremiah18:7 AMP).

So, the big question in the context of taking dictation is: "Can we put our trust in the words of one who is unchangeable in character but flexible in his interactions with us?" I believe it is possible if we can grasp the incredible hugeness of God that is revealed in this open view of the future.

Perfection Looks Different In a Person

One of the problems in adopting the definition of perfection that was handed down from Plato is that while it is a very sound definition when applied to inanimate things – a perfect mathematical formula, by definition, is one that cannot be improved or diminished – a perfect work of art is one that needs no improving strokes or redrawing of lines. But when it's applied to a living being this definition doesn't always make sense. For example, if it were possible for a person to be perfect in that way, we would expect a state of mind that cannot be changed through interaction with others. But what would we think of a person, filled with joy, who walked past a suffering beggar and did not allow that situation to change his state of mind or even his plans for the day? What would we think of a builder who refused to make changes in his building in order to correct structural mistakes that had been made by the contractors?

When it comes to living beings, perfection is not defined as being unchangeable but as being willing to change for the good of others.

A good example of this in the Bible is in Genesis 6:5-6 where it says, "The Lord saw how great the wickedness of the human race had become on the earth, and that every inclination of the thoughts of the human heart was only evil all the time. The Lord regretted that he had made human beings on the earth, and his heart was deeply troubled." Is it really possible to regret something that turned out exactly as you knew it would turn out? Does it not make more sense to believe that God's plans for the human race were affected by their interaction with the choices of human beings, causing God to "reboot" through the line of Noah? Another example of this is in I Samuel 15:11 where God said to the prophet Samuel, "I regret that I have made Saul king, because he has turned away from me and has not carried out my instructions." You can see in those words that if Saul had not turned away from God there was the probability that he could have been a good king, God regretted the fact that Saul's free will had changed the plans that God had for his future!

As we'll see in a moment, this doesn't mean that God has no control over the future and is wringing his hands, wondering what mankind is going to do next, but Scriptures like this do show us that there is a flexibility in the way that God interacts with us and makes plans for our lives. The very fact that we are urged to pray in places like I Timothy 2: 1-4 where it says, "...I urge that supplications, prayers, intercessions, and thanksgivings be made for all people, for kings and all who are in high positions, that we may lead a peaceful and quiet life, godly and dignified in every way. This is good, and it is pleasing in the sight of God our Savior, who desires all people to be saved and to come to the knowledge of the truth," demonstrates that God's desire for all people to be saved does not mean they will all be saved, but their choices and futures are influenced by our prayers. To pray for people whose future is already settled would be a colossal waste of time, but if their future is flexible through their choices, then prayer becomes a much more serious endeavor!

In terms of taking dictation, this means that we keep a journal of God's words and promises always with the understanding that the working out of those plans can be affected by interactions with the will of others, just as God's promise to Samuel concerning Saul then changed and found its fulfillment in David. As we will see next, this doesn't limit our view of God's sovereignty but greatly expands it!

God Is Greater Than a Preordained Future

In his excellent lecture entitled: 'Flexible Sovereignty: An Open View of the Future,' Dr. Greg Boyd[5] pointed out that an open view of the future paints a much *bigger* portrait of God. He makes the important point that God does indeed know all things, but all things include future possibilities. God settles whatever he chooses ahead of time, but he also opens up possibilities ahead of time to whatever extent he chooses. For example, back in the 60s, there was a popular series of books for young adults called *Choose Your Own Adventure*. You would read along in the story until you came to a choice: 1) Young Billy could go fishing with his friends to the creek 2) Young Billy could go into the old mine or 3) Young Billy could go into the abandoned house. Where the adventure went next depended on the choice you made. The author treated each choice as a certainty and had worked out the storyline completely, but the direction the adventure took was up to the reader.

---

[5] Boyd, G. (2015). Video retrieved in 2019 from: https://www.youtube. com/watch?v=SyZQySJeg4g

A deeper explanation can be found in his book, *God of the Possible*. (2000). US: Baker Books.

It is said that most world-level masters in chess can visualize thirty moves ahead of whatever move their opponent might make on a chessboard. Even though that displays a remarkable degree of intelligence, our God is infinitely intelligent and so can anticipate every possible move we might make and have a plan that he has been anticipating since the foundation of eternity. The truth is that an open future view does not limit God, but greatly expands our appreciation of the unlimited intelligence of God!

In his lecture, Boyd also pointed out that this understanding of God makes him much more praiseworthy. In another chess example, let's suppose that one player wins a chess game while playing against a computer that he has programmed and completely controls. Another player wins a chess game while playing against a computer using a script that tells him every move the computer will make. A third player wins a chess game while playing against a computer simply because he is smarter than the computer. Which of the three players is praiseworthy? It takes no intelligence to win against an opponent that you control, or even against an opponent where you know every move, so only the player that won on his own merit is worthy of acclamation. When we realize that God is not just going through the motions while following a static future that is already decided but is instead able to make a perfect plan for every probability, we discover that he is truly worthy of our praise!

A good example of this in the Bible is when God shared with Moses that he would lead his people out of slavery in Egypt. He promised Moses that the people would listen to him in Exodus 3:18, but in the next chapter, Moses brought up the question of another probability: "Then Moses answered and said, 'But suppose they will not believe me or listen to my voice; suppose they say, 'The Lord has not appeared to you.' So the Lord said to him, 'What is in your hand?' He said, 'A rod.' And he said, 'Cast it on the ground.' So he cast it on the ground and it became a serpent; and Moses fled from it" (Exodus 4:1-3 NKJV). Notice that God didn't say, "It's already settled that they will listen to you so don't worry about it," but instead pointed out that he had the probability they wouldn't listen covered as well, with the miracle of the rod.

Within the context of taking dictation, this understanding helps us to realize that God is not limited to a prewritten script, for even if things go in a different direction from what he had originally promised, he has a fully formed plan for that possibility as well and is willing to show us what he intends to do. I don't believe that I missed God when he told us back in Russia to buy the Mir Theater. Instead, the city fathers just chose of their own free will to not accept our offer, and eventually we found that God had covered that probability by giving us an excellent church meeting place located on a busy street in Perm, Russia.

It's hard to find the motivation to listen to God every morning if we believe that everything in our day is preordained and unchangeable. That kind of quiet time is more out of a sense of duty rather than a sense of discovery. But if we believe that the sovereignty of God is flexible as he interacts with his creation and if we can begin to see a divine intelligence able to treat every probability as a certainty, then taking dictation becomes one of the most exciting and important aspects of our Christian walk.

Surprises Strengthen Relationships

People who are in strong and mature marriage relationships will tell you that the real purpose of marriage is not to make you happy, but to make you holy! The surprises and even disappointments that occur as two people attempt to be one flesh have a way of shaping and molding character in a way that nothing else can. All relationships have this same basic purpose, including our relationship with God. If he had wanted to, God could have created a very predictable human existence where there were no surprises and we would be happy all the time, but above all else, our heavenly Father desires that we grow, and growth only comes when we are shaped by the unexpected.

We must always remember that at the core of everything that God does we find the foundational principle of relationship. When asked what was the greatest commandment from God, Jesus immediately said it was loving God and loving your neighbor, and then he went on to point out that all religion (which he summarized in Matthew 22:40 as the "law and the prophets") hangs on those two principles! When teaching his disciples to pray, Jesus never mentioned the technique of prayer but instead started his model of prayer in the context of relationship: "Our Father in heaven" (Matthew 6:9). When we are attempting to take dictation in our quiet time each morning, we must always remember that God's ultimate purpose for our life is not that we have an inside track on knowing his will or even good feelings to carry us through the day, but that we have a relationship that is deep enough to withstand every storm in life. The real test of any relationship is not how we respond to blessings, but how we respond to surprises.

From the time of God's promise to make Abraham a great nation until the actual birth of his son Isaac was an astounding period of three decades! Abraham made mistakes during that time and even tried to fulfill that promise himself through Ishmael, yet when the unexpected happened and he was asked to sacrifice the promised child as a burnt offering, we discover the kind of relationship that had developed between Abraham and his God during those three decades. When Isaac asked where the lamb was for the burnt offering, Abraham answered, "God himself will provide the lamb for the burnt offering my son" (Genesis 22:8). We are shown later in the New Testament that Abraham's trust in the goodness and character of God was greater than what seemed to be contradictions in what he was hearing from God. In Hebrews 11:19, it says, "Abraham reasoned that God could even raise the dead, and so in a manner of speaking he did receive Isaac back from death." Three decades of waiting, which included times of confusion in interpreting the promise, as well as words that seem to contradict the promise, did not destroy Abraham's faith; on the contrary, it created a faith that could believe God was able to raise the dead!

Because we live in a universe where a perfect God chooses to interact and be influenced by those he has created, it should underline even more the necessity of constant communication with him. And when surprises come our way, the key to weathering them (and even growing because of them) is to remember that God is not just following a preordained script. Yet he knows all things, even all probabilities, and has a plan that he has created from the foundation of the world!

Questions to Ponder

1. What can your reaction to surprises tell you about the maturity of your relationship with God?

2. Can you give further examples of how the definition of perfection is different between inanimate and animate objects?

3. In what ways does an open view of the future paint a bigger portrait of God?

4. Can you give some examples of how unexpected difficulties can shape your life in a positive way?

5. Have there been times in your life where things have gone differently from what you felt God had promised? What was your reaction in those times?

Chapter Eleven

Making Room for His Word

Coming to Jesus in 1976, at the age of 23, was the most exciting thing that had ever happened to me in my young life. A latecomer to the counterculture movement and all things "hippie" in Birmingham, Alabama, I had still dedicated myself in the previous three years to a lifestyle that brought me perilously close to the edge of drug addiction and crime. In the early summer of that year, I was gripped by a strong and inexplicable desire to travel and to see America. So, accompanied by a somewhat older hippie friend, I hitchhiked across the country from Alabama to Northern California. There was still a strong hippie tribal culture in the 70s and we had no real problems finding rides and places to stay on our journey. After two weeks, we ended up in the small Northern California community of Dunsmuir, a picturesque little town located on the headwaters of the Sacramento River just beneath the towering snow-peaked Mount Shasta. The first people we met were "Jesus Freaks" (as they were called in those days), former hippies who had given their lives to following Jesus. Even though I had been raised in a nominal kind of Christianity, I had never encountered anything like this and by the end of my very first day in Northern California, I had become a "Jesus Freak" myself!

While many in the body of Christ today might raise an eyebrow at some of the excesses of the Jesus movement, we really were dedicated to a Christian counterculture with Jesus at the center. I was fortunate to have a compassionate and godly pastor who directed many of us through that time, so our lives were filled with only one purpose: to tell others about Jesus Christ. I flinch a little today when I think about the way I would corner people on the street with my tracts and my very sketchy understanding of the Gospel, but the amazing thing was that in those years we saw many hundreds of people come to Jesus! I played harmonica in a local Christian band and we would set up our equipment anywhere there were non-Christian people; and even though our music was a little raw, there were many who were touched by the Holy Spirit as they sat in parks and listened to our testimonies.

After the death of my father, I returned to Alabama, working in a big furniture factory and bringing my former "Jesus Freak" zeal to the local Pentecostal church. But I began to notice that it was becoming harder to hear the Lord's direction, and in my lifestyle, I had started to compromise a bit as a single man in my relationships with others. It finally all came to a point where I realized that the problem was not that I had become empty, it was that I had become too full! I had been a Christian for a few years now and I was filled with the knowledge of how to do church and teach Sunday school and be involved in my church in countless ways (at one point, I led the choir, directed the children's church, and drove the church van every Sunday)! It seemed as though I had no more room left for anything new that Jesus might want to say to me. This understanding led me to the decision to leave my job and church in Alabama and enroll in a full-time five-month school called the Discipleship Training School, which is the entry-level school of an amazing mission organization called Youth with a Mission. What I learned there was not just missionary training, but discipleship training: that I had to make a lot of room for the character that God wanted to build in my life!

It's interesting that Jesus used this same kind of language when he spoke to the large number of Pharisees who had begun to attend his teachings, some even becoming believers. In John 8:37 he said,

"I know that you are Abraham's descendants. Yet you are looking for a way to kill me, because you have no room for my word." I find it fascinating that the reason they opposed Jesus to the point of wanting to kill him was not that they were evil men or even politicians who were connected with the Roman government, these men were the religious leaders of their community, but they had come to the point where they had no more room for God's word! To me, this is the great tragedy of the Pharisees: for generations they had protected the nation of Israel against the influence of Greek philosophy and conquering nations; they had preserved the Word of God by duplicating exact copies of the Torah, but when God had something new to say through Jesus, they had no room in their hearts and minds to receive it.

I believe that this phenomenon also happens today in the lives of Christians who have been following Jesus for a while, and it's easy to misinterpret our inability to hear anything new to mean either: 1) "There are no more new things to hear, so I'll focus on codifying the old," or 2) "I just need to get busier doing the work of the Lord and I will get through this dry time." But could it be that there is a third explanation: that we will not hear anything new until we've made room for the new?

It's significant that the New Testament points out that Jesus, when he came to Earth, had to go through a very similar process of making room. In Philippians 2:6–7 (ESV), it says, "though he was in the form of God, did not count equality with God a thing to be grasped, but emptied himself, by taking the form of a servant, being born in the likeness of men." Jesus made it clear throughout his life that the Son only does what he hears from the Father, and it's noteworthy that to be in that place of hearing the Father's words, he had to first empty himself when taking on the likeness of men.

What does it mean to make room for his Word? I don't believe it means that we reject the core theology of Christianity that binds all Christians into the body of Christ, but it does mean something! When Jesus said to the Pharisees, "You have no room for my word," the implication was that they could have made room if they had wanted to. Remember that most of the Pharisees were not filled with demons or sin, they were filled with traditions and worship styles and interpretations of Scripture going back for generations. So, let's explore what it means to make room for more of his word.

To Make Room We Must Re-Examine Our Religion

The Oxford Dictionary definition of religion is: "the belief in and worship of a superhuman controlling power, especially a personal God or gods." Even though this is a good generic way to describe most religions, there is a very important distinction that we must re-examine when it comes to the Christian religion. Am I religious in order to please God and gain admittance into his kingdom, or am I (as a Christian) religious because Jesus has already made a way for me in his kingdom and is already pleased with me? Most of the Pharisees were so committed to that first concept of religion, so filled with its rules and principles, that they were not only unable to recognize the Messiah, they were ready to kill him!

Religion has a way of filling our lives and crowding out everything, even the normal empathy and emotions that human beings are born with. One of the most shocking examples of this is in John chapter 9, which is the story of the healing of the man who had been blind from birth. Jesus had already broken several religious rules by putting a mixture of spit and mud into the poor man's eyes, then commanding him to go to the pool of Siloam on the most important day of the Festival of Tabernacles – all on the Sabbath, when you are not supposed to work! But notice that when the Pharisees heard about the miracle, there is no mention (not one word) of their joy in hearing that a member of their community had been healed of blindness. Instead, they had only one concern, in John 9:15, "Therefore the Pharisees also asked him how he had received his sight." This concern that his healing be in line with their religion was so all-consuming that they questioned the man, they questioned his parents, then questioned the man again – and at the end of this interrogation, they kicked him out of church! Religion had crowded out all empathy, even the normal human reaction of joy in seeing someone relieved of a lifetime of suffering.

So, what does it mean to re-examine religion in order to make room? It doesn't mean that we, necessarily, challenge the denomination that we are a part of, or come up with exotic theology that's never been heard before... it means a re-examination of the way that we *use* religion. The Pharisees didn't need to reject the Torah, for it had always pointed to the Messiah, they needed to take a second look at how they were using the Torah in their attempts to worship God. Long before the coming of Jesus, God was pleading for his people to re-examine their religion when he said in Isaiah 29:13, "These people come near to me with their mouth and honor me with their lips, but their hearts are far from me. Their worship of me is based on merely human rules they have been taught." This is a human tendency that goes far beyond the Pharisees: we have a personal encounter with God, and we worship him because of that encounter, but gradually the *way* we worship becomes more important than the one whom we are worshiping. As a pastor, I've counseled many people whose only word from the Lord was something they heard twenty years ago as teenagers; their lives are filled with church activities and Bible studies and good works, but like the Pharisees, their worship is more based now on the religious process than a fresh encounter with God. (Remember the moldy bread!)

Re-examining religion is not rejecting our Christianity but recognizing this tendency of religion to fill up our lives; and when we see that this has occurred, we must be willing to examine the things in our lives that perhaps are due for a spring clean. For some, that might mean a re-examination of my values. If my values are determined by what I put my time, energy, and money into, then how valuable is my personal relationship with God? If all my time, energy, and money is going into the practice of Christianity with little time, energy or money left for my relationship with Christ, then I need a realignment of those values in my life.

For others that might mean a re-examination of where I place my faith: if my faith rests on the theory of creationism versus evolution or the rapture or dispensationalism, then I must honestly ask myself, "Is this an authentic faith that lines up with what the Bible says about faith?" In Romans 10:17 (NKJV), it states, "So then faith comes by hearing, and hearing by the word of God." The Pharisees placed such great faith in their tradition they had no room left for faith in Jesus. Making room for God's word is not just a mental exercise, sometimes it is a realignment of how we spend our time and where we place our priorities.

To Make Room We Must Die To Self

One of the difficulties in trying to clear out the old stuff as I described above, is that it has a frustrating tendency to sneak back in! Perhaps I make a decision to realign my values, but slowly the old values begin to reassert themselves; I determine not to put my faith in religious traditions, but gradually my dependence upon them is reestablished. I think that Jesus understood this human tendency and that's why he gave what is perhaps the most important principle to really following him throughout our lives. In Luke 9:23 he said, "If anyone would come after me, let him deny himself and take up his cross daily and follow me." The phrase "come after me" in the Greek means to follow closely behind him, and it's interesting that what enables us to follow him through our lives is not the purity of our theology or our experience as churchgoers – but our willingness to deny self and daily pick up the cross!

Although it's popular in Christian circles to talk about some difficult experience as "the cross I have to bear"; to the crowd who heard Jesus say those words, the cross was a clear and unequivocal reference to only one thing – death! It's really quite shocking if you take literally the preconditions that Jesus laid down for following him: that we will never be able to really effectively follow (hearing his directions and going where he goes) unless we are willing to die to ourselves!

So, the natural question that arises is, "What does it mean to die to self?" Most people understand that it means "to present your body as a living sacrifice" (Romans 12:1 ESV), but in the letter that Paul wrote to the Galatian church, a church that was being tempted to turn back to some of the religious practices of Judaism, we see a deeper explanation of what it means to die to self. In Galatians 2:20, he said, "I have been crucified with Christ and I no longer live, but Christ lives in me. The life I now live in the body, I live by faith in the Son of God, who loved me and gave himself for me." This is much more than just a willingness to sacrifice things for Jesus – to be crucified with Christ meant two very distinctive things to Paul:

I No Longer Live But Christ Lives In Me

Obviously, after Paul gave his heart to Jesus he continued to live and breathe, but the source of his life and his sense of value and purpose had completely died, and now his source of life was Christ living in him! This is a very different way of looking at our relationship with Jesus: he is not just the means by which I was saved or the one who wants to bless my day, he is my life and in him, I find the meaning of life! If I can't really say that about Jesus, then I must face the fact that I haven't really, this day, taken up my cross! Jesus made it clear that death to self was not just a one-shot deal that happened when I became a Christian, but a daily practice of deliberately choosing to find my life in him and in nothing else but him!

The Life I Now Live I Live By Faith In The Son

Life requires that I be willing to put my faith in something: for many, it is faith in the fact that I will have a job in the morning or the means to pay my bills, or a society that will continue to protect me and meet my needs. But for Paul, new life required that he daily put his faith in Jesus. Not just faith for salvation, but faith in the fact that Jesus is the revelation of everything that he needed to live his life – a revelation of what it means to live as a son of the Father; a revelation of how to relate to others in his society; a revelation of the heart and character of God himself. Paul was able to live a life of faith in Jesus because he understood that in Jesus all things are revealed!

I've come to believe that this was what Jesus was talking about when he said in Mark 8:35, "For whoever would save his life will lose it, but whoever loses his life for my sake and the Gospels will save it." To lose your life for his sake is not just referring to martyrdom, but to be willing to bring to the altar everything in life that you are living for and choose instead to live every day for his sake and the Gospel's sake.

One of the great tragedies of the modern church is that we have substituted a works-centered Christianity for a death-centered Christianity, trying to follow Jesus by our own efforts instead of embracing the precondition that to follow him I must deny myself!

To Make Room We Must Be Willing To Be Pruned

My father grew up as a sharecropper's son in rural Arkansas in the depths of the Great Depression. Serving in World War II gave him the opportunity to go to college (the first in his family ever to do so) and even though he had a career as a civil engineer, he bought a "gentleman's farm" later in life, which included a small orchard of pear trees. At a certain time of the season, he had to do something to those trees that, at first glance, seemed counterproductive in the eyes of his city-boy son: he had to go out to where those trees were growing, spread their branches, and then cut those branches back to the point where they were not nearly so big or beautiful as they had been before! From his agricultural background, he understood that fruit trees have to be pruned for two important reasons: 1) Pruning back branches improves sunlight penetration and increases the air movement throughout the tree, and 2) Pruning causes branches to multiply, developing a structure within the tree that can support a load of fruit.

Jesus pointed to this correlation between fruitfulness and making room in a parable that he gave in John 15:1-2, "I am the true vine, and my Father is the gardener. He cuts off every branch in me that bears no fruit, while every branch that does bear fruit, he prunes so that it will be even more fruitful." There was a time some years ago when I was reading this parable and I felt God say to my heart, "Son, do you want to be a big tree or a fruitful tree? You can't always be both." Up until that point, I had always assumed that God's highest intention for my ministry was that it would become bigger and bigger, but I was facing a time in my life where it was about to become decidedly smaller. I didn't fully understand why it was happening, but looking back, I can now see that my branches needed to be pruned back in order to increase the movement of the wind of the Holy Spirit throughout my life, as well as to create a structure that could bear fruit in the future.

There is much in our Western "big box" culture that keeps us in a place where we have no room for God's word. Success is always measured by size, but there comes a time in every person's life when size crowds out fruitfulness. It's easy to run from the gardener's pruning shears in modern Christianity: we can convince ourselves that it is the enemy trying to limit us, we can leave one project and start trying to build another project. But the truth is that there are many times in our lives where less will bring more if we're willing to trust the gardener. I find it interesting that on some level John the Baptist understood this principle when he said in John 3:30, "He must become greater; I must become less." We tend to read that as though John was sadly declaring the end of his usefulness for God, but John understood that for the word of Jesus to increase, John's words would have to decrease.

As a pastor who has been around other pastors for thirty years, I am constantly amazed at how little time many leaders spend listening for the words and direction of God. There is something about the "big tree" of church ministry that becomes so all-encompassing there is little time left to simply sit quietly before God and give him the best parts of our day. The Pharisees had a big tree in their attempts to preserve the Torah and to guide the religious life of Israel, but we must never forget that their unwillingness to be pruned led to their inability to hear or receive the words of the Messiah when he came!

In the seasons of our lives when we have lost touch a bit in our relationship with God, it's tempting to want to go back and do what we did before (only harder!) but the truth is that holding on to our cluttered collection of religious principles does not have the effect of hearing the new things that God wants to speak to us. When Jesus said to the Pharisees, "You have no room for my word," I believe that he was speaking to every person who had been following him for a while. That statement should not shame us, but fill us with great hope, for although I may not be able to always do more for Jesus, I can certainly do less! I can clean out some of the religion in my life and realize that what God needs is not always just a busy laborer, but an empty vessel that he can fill!

Questions to Ponder

1. What are some examples of things, both secular and religious, that can fill up your life to the point where you have no room for God's words?

2. Think about the two reasons why people choose to be religious: what is the great difference between using religion to please God and being religious because he is already pleased?

3. When religion is used in the wrong way, why does it crowd out love and empathy for others? Are there some examples in modern church life where we see this phenomenon?

4. We all understand that we are to die to our sinful self, but what does it mean to die to all of myself? Are there some things that I trust in that must be brought to the altar as a living sacrifice?

5. Why do we so often try to avoid the Heavenly Gardener's pruning shears? What does it mean to you to choose to be a fruitful tree rather than a bigger tree?

Chapter Twelve

What Now?

Just a few years after giving my heart to Jesus, I was amazed at how much my life had changed: I had quickly transitioned from hippie to "Jesus freak" to Sunday school teacher and then, as a member of a Pentecostal church in my home state of Alabama, I had been asked to be the children's church director, which in that church was a solo position – me and more than 30 kids!

God had given me a big heart for my kids, and I struggled in the first few months to try to understand just what I wanted to accomplish as a pastor over children. Was my goal only to keep them occupied or entertained while the main service was going on upstairs? What could I do to build a foundation in their lives that would take them from childhood into their adult years? It was at that time I came across a book that has had a lasting influence on my understanding of teaching, *Creative Bible Teaching*[6] by Lawrence Richards. Along with giving me a structure for teaching that I have used to this day (hook, book, look, took), Dr. Richards also pointed out that teaching is only creative if you can do more than just hook someone's attention, or open their understanding of God's book, or even look and see how those truths apply to their lives. According to him, teaching is only creative if you can guide someone to the "took" stage where they actually *respond* by taking that truth and incorporating it into their lives!

My desire in writing this book is to do more than just hook you with stories from the mission field or even to show you what God's

---

[6] Richards, L.O., Bredfeldt, G.J. (1998). *Creative Bible Teaching*. USA: Moody Publishers. It was originally published in 1970.

book says about his desire to speak. It is to inspire you to take the evidence that I've tried to present and then respond by starting a daily regimen of taking dictation. I would like to "boil down" this book into some practical steps that enable you to start this process tomorrow morning when you have turned the final page of this book.

Step #1: Have Faith That God Wants To Speak To You

There are many things in our lives that we have faith in, even when we don't understand exactly how they work. I have faith that the lights will come on when I flip the light switch (although that faith is tested sometimes in foreign lands). I have faith that when the "walk" sign comes on at a busy intersection in Atlanta, that the traffic will stop, and I can safely walk across. That faith is based on my conviction that the electric power plant will be faithful in operating today, and that people will be faithful in obeying the traffic signals. In that same way, it's important to allow the evidence that we have of God speaking in the Bible to convince us that he has always done it, even if we don't know exactly how, and he wants to continue faithfully speaking to his children.

In our relationship with God, it is important to turn away from habits we may have developed as young Christians that are based upon our doubt that God can guide us with his voice. Shortcuts such as depending primarily on circumstances or feelings might have been sufficient when we were brand-new followers, but there comes a time pretty quickly when God wants us to grow up into mature followers who are able to hear his direction. It's not that shortcuts are, in and of themselves sinful, the problem is that they are too easy! If we want to grow closer in our relationship with God, we must accept the fact that all relationships require the learning of new skills and the reordering of priorities.

It's important to remember that God, from the beginning of creation, has always used the tool of words. Part of faith is to submit to this fact and not to insist that God communicates with you in some different way. He doesn't want to just pour confidence into your life like a commodity, he wants to give you confidence by speaking the encouraging words of a Father. He doesn't want to hand you a map of your life, he wants to go with you as your guide, taking the same steps that you take and speaking words of direction when they are needed. He will not just strengthen your life out of thin air, he wants you to understand that man can only live by every word that proceeds from the mouth of God!

Step #2: Give God an Opportunity To Speak

One of the most effective falsehoods that the enemy has ever spoken to Christians is the idea that "if God wants to speak to me, he will speak." Like so many of the enemy's lies, it is a half-truth, God does want to speak to me, but he will not (except in a dire emergency) overpower my will and drown out every other voice in my life! Along with the evidence that we have in the Bible that God chooses to use the tool of words, we also have evidence of the *way* he uses that tool: with a still small voice. And even though that might seem unfair when you first think about it, you begin to realize that there is a loving reason why God speaks softly: he wants us to draw near!

If you are going to follow Dr. Richard's definition of what it means to be creative, it means there must be a willingness to respond to this book by making a small alteration to your schedule in the morning when you start your day. Determine in your heart that, along with whatever else you do in your quiet time, you will set aside ten minutes each morning with a pen in your hand and an open page in a notebook to give God the opportunity to speak back to you. People who are visually wired might write a sentence describing an image that is in their mind, while others might describe an impression that is in their hearts. God speaks in different ways, but he will only speak if we give him the opportunity to speak!

Part of giving God opportunity also requires that we be willing to alter the way that we read the Bible: not just looking for answers to our questions but also allowing the Bible to question us! Because, by and large, the human race has forgotten what the voice of God sounds like, we must tune our ears once more to his voice by letting him speak to us through his written word. Remember that this requires a willingness to not only look *at* the written word analytically, but to also look *along* the word of God (in the same way that C.S. Lewis looked along the beam of light in the dark toolshed) – allowing God's word to change our paradigm of the world.

A confident and assured lifestyle does not come to a Christian through knowing everything that will happen in life, but from the knowledge that if I have given him an opportunity to speak, he will be faithful, in his time, to show me what I should do!

Step #3: Allow The Holy Spirit To Work

The honest truth is that taking dictation is impossible if we are not willing to allow the Holy Spirit to perform his role in our lives. Jesus made this perfectly clear when he said in John 16:13, "When the Spirit of truth comes, he will guide you into all the truth, for he will not speak on his own authority, but whatever he hears he will speak, and he will declare to you the things that are to come." The Holy Spirit has a much greater role than just miracles among other people, his gifts are also meant to be applied to ourselves! Jesus made a tremendous promise when he said those words, a promise that has been largely unrealized among Christians in the 21st-century. If you believe in such things as prophecy and words of knowledge and words of wisdom, then understand that it is by using these gifts that God wants to speak to you.

Oftentimes we see things like quiet times and journaling as a matter of having greater self-discipline, but in the past thirty years, I've discovered that just the opposite is true: hearing God is not a matter of taking hold of yourself, but a matter of dying to yourself and making room for the words of God that the Holy Spirit wants to speak into your heart. When God said to the apostle Paul that his strength is made perfect in weakness, it wasn't a glorification of weaknesses but a recognition that we must not lean on our own understanding or strength if we are going to hear God better – we must lean on the Helper that he has sent us, his Holy Spirit!

Step #4: Desire Character More Than Information

I've always found it interesting that the apostle James said in James 4:2–3, "You do not have because you do not ask God. When you ask, you do not receive, because you ask with wrong motives…" In other words, we don't see things happen in our lives because we're not dialoguing with God, but even when we are in dialogue with him, what we are asking for is hindered by our motives! There is a real danger in seeing taking dictation only as a way to have an "edge" or an inside track in how to operate our lives or ministry which, if we're not extremely careful, can put us into the same category as those who practice spiritualism or other forms of magic. Hearing from God is much less about "what do you want me to do" as "who do you want me to become?" When Jesus talked about the kinds of people that inhabit the kingdom of God, he never mentioned the most educated or even the most religious; instead, he talked about character traits, such as becoming like a little child or choosing to be a servant of all.

The greatest motivation that we can have to take dictation and keep a prayer journal is the understanding that only the words of the Father can give us a true sense of who we are and what our value really is. Only the light that is generated by his words can illuminate areas in our lives that he wants to mold and shape, and only when we gaze upon his glory in his word can we be transformed into that same glory!

We must never forget that, after taking off the old man at the moment of our salvation, what enables us to put on the new man has to be changed in the attitude of our minds (paraphrased from Ephesians 4:23-24). Listening to God's word for us is meant to do much more than just give directions, it is meant to change the way we think! As our way of thinking lines up with God's, we can gradually become that new person God intends us to be!

Step #5: Be Determined To Obey

To obey really is better than sacrifice! (See I Samuel 15:22). This means that what pleases the heart of God is not how much time a person spends in quiet time, but how willing that person is to make decisions based upon what he or she is hearing from God. It has been my habit in the past twenty years to regularly go back and review the entries that I've made in my prayer journal. Almost without exception, I've discovered things the Lord asked me to do that in the rush of a busy life I had forgotten about. It has also been my habit as a leader and a pastor to try not to get caught up in some good idea but to create a "prayer buffer" by waiting for God to confirm the next move before making it.

Even though I might not be as quick to obey as I should be, I firmly believe that if God sees a determination in my heart to obey what he speaks to me in my journal, he will be encouraged to speak more. We must never forget that just hearing God's word does not build the sure foundation that he wants us to have in our lives, it is only when we hear his word and then put it into practice!

What Now?
Step #1: Have faith that God wants to speak to you
Step #2: Give God an opportunity to speak
Step #3: Allow the Holy Spirit to work
Step #4: Desire character more than information
Step #5: Be determined to obey

What we do next is more important than we realize

We are living in a time in the 21st century where there is a real danger that God's people will forget that we are meant to be the sheep of his pasture. It's easy to go our own way and to embrace a religious Christianity instead of a lifestyle where we are determined to actually follow Christ. It is my prayer that this book has opened your heart to the fact that God is still speaking today, and he is still determined to use words to transform our inner lives, as well as the ministry that he's called us to perform.

If you are willing to set the bar low at first, and value consistency in daily taking dictation over quantity, I am convinced that you will discover a greater and greater ability to hear what God is saying and to embrace the lifestyle of Jesus, who could do nothing by himself, but only what he heard and saw the Father doing around him – these are the people who will change the world!

53653251R00100